SOUTHEAST ASIA

THE THIRD WORLD SERIES

 AFRICA

 LATIN AMERICA

 MIDDLE EAST

 SOUTH ASIA

 SOUTHEAST ASIA

THE THIRD WORLD

SOUTHEAST ASIA

Donald K. Swearer

The Dushkin Publishing Group, Inc.
Guilford, Connecticut 06437

Library of Congress Catalog Card Number: 84-92909

Manufactured in the United States of America.

First Printing

CONTENTS

SOUTHEAST ASIA

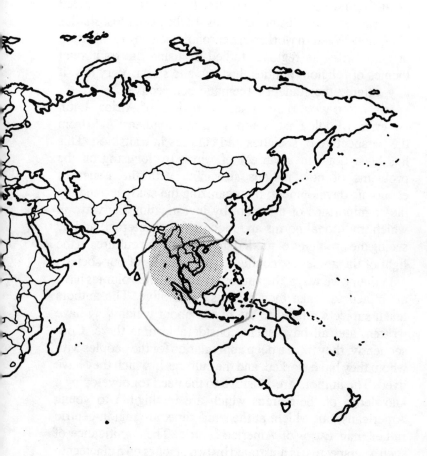

FOREWORD

THE THIRD WORLD has been written to provide much needed materials on non-Western cultures. In the past, most studies of the non-Western world were chronological in organization or dealt with the regions studied by using the traditional themes of religion, politics, history, and so on. Very few, if any, offered the student a thematic perspective.

THE THIRD WORLD discusses the regions of Africa, Latin America, Middle East, South Asia, and Southeast Asia from the perspective of societies and cultures in transition. This has been done in a variety of ways: by focusing on the problems of new nations struggling with the issues of economic development; by organizing the study around the major minorities of a region; by investigating the ways in which traditional norms and modern forms interact; and by seeing the problems of modern non-American cultures in the light of the anxieties, conflicts, and tensions of our society.

In their own ways, the authors of each of the volumes have attempted to make their regions come alive. The authors teach subjects related to the region about which they have written, and all have spent considerable time there. Consequently, they have a deep appreciation for the peoples with whom they have worked, and the cultures in which they have lived. The authors are sensitive to the need for developing a knowledge of their areas which are intelligible to young Americans, but which, at the same time, are region-centric rather than Euro- or America-centric. The significance of such a perspective is illustrated by two plaques on a nineteenth century Spanish monument on the island of Mactan in the

Philippines glorifying God, Spain, the Queen Regent then in power, and Ferdinand Magellan. In 1941 a historical marker titled, "Ferdinand Magellan's Death" was anchored into the monument stating, "On this spot Ferdinand Magellan died on April 27, 1521, wounded in an encounter with the soldiers of Lapulapu, Chief of Mactan island. One of Magellan's ships, the Victoria, under the command of Juan Sebastian Elcano, sailed from Cebu on May 1, 1521, and anchored at San Lucar de Barrameda on September 6, 1522, thus completing the first circumnavigation of the earth." Ten years later, in 1951, the newly independent Republic of the Philippines erected a second marker entitled "Lapulapu." It read, "Here, on 27 April 1521, Lapulapu and his men repulsed the Spanish invaders, killing their leader Ferdinand Magellan. Thus, Lapulapu became the first Filipino to have repelled European aggression."

The authors of the volumes of THE THIRD WORLD are not only interested in these countries from an academic point of view. They also hope to be able to make a contribution to world understanding and world peace by increasing your knowledge of non-Western cultures, peoples, and societies.

THE THIRD WORLD has, in short, been written with a sense of urgency and a sense of mission. The urgency is the chaotic state of today's world. The mission is knowledge, not the kind of knowledge that comes from memorizing facts, but the understanding that comes from dispelling myths and from grappling with problems relevant to you and the world in which you live. You have a stake in the future of the world. It's a rapidly shrinking world in which the problems of the Third World are your problems. It's up to you to try to solve them. We hope that THE THIRD WORLD will be of some help along the way.

—**Donald K. Swearer**
Editorial Advisor
Third World Series
Swathmore College

ABOUT THE AUTHOR

Donald K. Swearer (B.A., M.A., Ph.D., Princeton University; B.D., S.T.M., Yale University Divinity School) has held teaching appointments at Oberlin College, the University of Pennsylvania, Harvard University, Princeton Theological Seminary, Bangkok Christian College, and is currently Professor of Asian Religions at Swarthmore College. He is the author of several books on Asian religion and culture including *Buddhism* (1977) and *Buddhism and Society in Southeast Asia* (1981). He was an assistant editor of the *Journal of Religious Ethics* and the *Journal of Ecumenical Studies*. He has spent several years living, studying, and teaching in Southeast Asia. He is a member of the Association for Asian Studies, the American Academy of Religion, the Siam Society, the American Society for the Study of Religion, and is on the board of the East-West Religions Project, the University of Hawaii.

INTRODUCTION

Until recent years, the area known as Southeast Asia was only vaguely familiar to most Americans. Yet, since at least 1965, this part of the world has demanded much of our attention. Our involvement in the Indo-China war claimed thousands of American lives and disrupted the economic and political fabric of our country. It was the most divisive event in American history since the Civil War.

The consequences of the Indo-China war might not have been so disastrous had we understood more about the whole of Southeast Asia—its history, culture, and peoples. This volume is intended to provide some knowledge about this region.

Southeast Asia is geographically, ethnically, and culturally diverse. Consequently, a volume this brief must be highly selective. I have addressed myself to those themes and problems which reflect my own deepest interests and background. While I have traveled extensively in Southeast Asia, I have spent the greatest amount of time in Thailand. As a result, this volume focuses on mainland Southeast Asia rather than the insular portions of the region, and it is more concerned with Buddhist Southeast Asia than those countries in which Islam and Christianity are the major religions.

ACKNOWLEDGEMENTS

I wish to thank Mrs. Edith Cohen, formerly of the stenographic office of Swarthmore College, who typed the manuscript for the original edition. I am very grateful to the Dushkin Publishing Group for their decision to publish a revised edition of The Third World Series.

1

THE COUNTRIES AND THEIR PEOPLES

Typical American tourists visiting Southeast Asia stop in Bangkok, Singapore, Manila, and, perhaps, Djakarta. They see large cities with some similarities to those at home and probably stay in an American-style hotel. Although they tour the local sights, their guides speak English, and as many conveniences as possible are provided for them. The tourists see the slums of these cities only by accident, and only special effort will break them away from air-conditioned comfort into the rural areas of Southeast Asia. At the end of the packaged Asian tour, tourists will probably have a series of memories so homogenized that none will have any distinctiveness. Thailand, Malaysia, Burma, Indonesia, and the Philippines will have melded together as Southeast Asia—a term hardly in use before World War II.

GEOGRAPHY AND CLIMATE

The part of the world called Southeast Asia is a diverse region geographically, ethnically, and culturally. It includes the Philippines, Indonesia, Singapore, Malaysia, Thailand, Laos, Kampuchea (formerly Cambodia), Vietnam, and Burma. These countries encompass both the mainland peninsula, sandwiched between India on the northwest and China on the northeast, and the two great island chains encircling more than half of this peninsula (see map on page 5). The location of Southeast Asia makes it a wall between the Indian and Pacific Oceans but also a land-sea

2

causeway between continental Asia and the islands of the Pacific like Australia. For this very reason it has been the focus of interchanges of peoples, cultures, religions, political ideologies, and commercial enterprises for hundreds of years.

The geography of Southeast Asia may be summarily characterized as "fragmented." The north-south trending mountains of mainland Southeast Asia divide the land into a series of compartments. Insular Southeast Asia is even more fragmented with thousands of islands extending over more than five thousand miles of ocean. Thus, unlike the North China Plain or the Indus-Ganges basin of India, Southeast Asia has no large core land area. As a consequence, its political history has been fragmented, having been dominated until the modern period by a series of diverse peoples who extended their power from varying geographic centers.

The mainland portion of the Southeast Asian region is guarded in the north by the mountain ranges and high plateaus of eastern Tibet and southwestern China. The peninsula itself is furrowed with major river systems flowing from the highlands in the northern portions to the sea—the Irrawaddy and Salween in Burma, the Menam Chao Praya in Thailand, and the mighty Mekong in Laos, Kampuchea, and Vietnam. The terrain is rugged. If you have ever hiked in the Appalachians, you will have some feeling for much of the land area of Southeast Asia, since about sixty percent is forested hills and mountains. On the other hand, if you have spent a summer in one of our delta areas like New Orleans, you will have an idea of the flat, alluvial plains in which are located major cities like Bangkok, Rangoon, and Saigon.

The island portions of Southeast Asia also are generally rugged. A few of the islands have volcanic cones rising as high as ten thousand feet above sea level. Some of the islands, like Sumatra, Borneo, Java, and New Guinea, rest on continental shelves and are fringed by shallow seas.

Others rise like pinnacles from the sea with practically no coastal plain.

Nearly all of Southeast Asia, mainland and islands alike, spreads across the equator in the hot, humid tropics marked by monsoon rains. Average sea-level temperature in all parts of Southeast Asia is about eighty degrees Fahrenheit. Temperatures vary seasonally, although one Bangkok resident once jestingly characterized the traditional dry, monsoon, and hot seasons of Central Thailand as "hot, hotter, and hottest!" Rainfall and temperature vary, yet much of Southeast Asia averages over sixty inches of annual rainfall.

While the relatively benign climate promotes luxuriant vegetation, soil in the upland regions, which comprises over eighty percent of the land area, is relatively poor. This soil supports forest growth more readily than field crops. Swidden or slash and burn agriculture, traditionally practiced in these areas, involves clearing forested plots and enriching the soil with ash from the burned timber. Yet, even with this kind of fertilization, after only a single crop season the land has to lie fallow for long periods. With population increases, the economic exploitation of the forests of Southeast Asia for export, and the prolonged political disruption of Indochina, rapid deforestation is jeopardizing the delicate ecological balance in many parts of the area. The loss of Southeast Asia's forests, furthermore, means not only the loss of trees and the erosion and depletion of soil, but threatens the storehouse of plant and animal species associated with the forest.

The lowland areas of Southeast Asia, the alluvial plains, comprise only about ten percent of the total land area. However, approximately ninety percent of the population lives in these areas. To improve these lowlands, Southeast Asians have developed various agricultural techniques to enhance productivity and allow for continuous cultivation. Foremost among these techniques has been the development of irrigated wet rice or paddy rice cultivation.

POLITICAL DIVISIONS OF SOUTHEAST ASIA

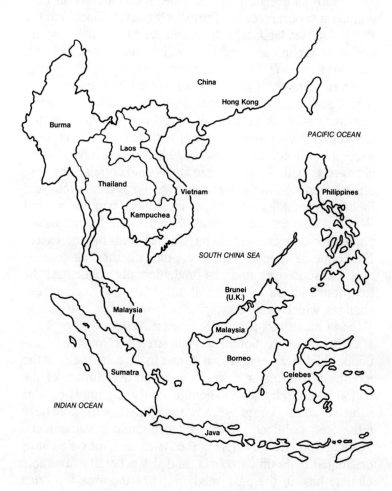

The countries of Southeast Asia (shown above) encompass many diverse and fragmented political and ethnic groups.

The traditional Southeast Asian economy was agricultural, subsistence farming. As one Southeast Asian geographer has observed, "A Burmese farmer dropped into the Philippine rice landscape three thousand miles away would find tools, techniques, and a way of life almost identical with that in Burma."[1] In the modern period beginning with Western merchantilism and colonialism, the economic picture of Southeast Asia has changed dramatically. Its mineral resources such as tin and oil have been sought after and developed. New crops for export such as coffee and rubber were introduced. Economic change brought about other changes as well. Alien Chinese and Indian populations were often introduced to work and manage large plantations and function as middlemen between indigenous populations and Western colonial rulers. With increasing industrialization population concentration in large urban areas has increased. Economic development along capitalistic lines has encouraged consumerism, and has fundamentally challenged the traditional ideals of the rural subsistence farmer. These changes, which came about gradually in Europe, have taken place in much less time in Southeast Asia.

Geographically, Southeast Asia stretches from the mountainous highlands of northern Burma to the delta plains at the mouths of the major rivers; and while the climate of the region is generally hot and humid, local geography provides some variation. The geography and climate of the area have influenced political, social, and economic developments. For example, rice, a staple of the Asian diet, may well have originated in Southeast Asia, and the generally favorable climate has, in the past, made parts of the area the "rice basket" of Asia. For this reason increased rice production in the United States may be looked upon with some alarm by rice exporting nations like Thailand.

ETHNIC UNITY AND DIVERSITY

The geography of Southeast Asia is a factor in the population density and ethnic composition of the region. Broad exposure to ocean on three sides and a mountainous border to the north have influenced the nature of the population and its development. Geography has made Southeast Asia a crossroads of peoples, cultures, and religions. It has also tended to limit population density on the peninsula. Population density is as diverse as our crowded coastal corridors in comparison to Montana or North Dakota. Yet, overall it averages over 185 people per square mile (1979 figure). China or India has over three times the population density. Populations have centered along the great river systems of the mainland peninsula, although various tribal groups settled in less hospitable, mountainous regions. This pattern is generally true today in countries like Burma, Thailand, and Laos. The insular areas have tended to be more crowded. The island of Java, for example, has one of the highest population densities in the world with an average of over one thousand persons per acre.

The peoples who have settled in this rich and fertile part of the world have many origins. The cultural foundations of Southeast Asia are thousands of years old. The earliest human inhabitants were related to the peoples who occupy the Pacific islands today—Negritos, Australoids, Melanesians. They lived in this region before the dawn of recorded history in what is known as the Pleistcene Age or Stone Age and left remains of stone, bone, pottery, and glass. At a later time a Mongolian type of people who finally came to dominate Southeast Asia introduced the use of metals, iron, and bronze and developed a finer and much wider variety of pottery. They are often referred to as the forerunners of the Malays or as Indonesian. In general terms this early prehistoric time, before the decisive influence of India, is referred to as the Austro-Asiatic Period of Southeast Asian culture.

During the Austro-Asiatic period, many practices, styles, and attitudes developed that are still important in large parts of Southeast Asia today, including the cultivation of paddy rice, the domestication of the ox and the buffalo, a social organization centered around irrigated cultivation, the veneration of ancestral spirits and gods of the soil, and the location of shrines on hillsides and mountain tops. Of course, this substratum did not continue through the ages in an unaltered form. It was decisively influenced by Indian culture beginning in the first and second centuries A.D. New ethnic groups like the Thais from southwestern China made fresh cultural contributions. In the thirteenth and fourteenth centuries, Islam began to make inroads into Southeast Asia and was particularly successful in the areas we now know as Indonesia and Malaysia. Finally, revolutionary changes in behavior, ideas, and attitudes accompanied an increasing Western presence during the nineteenth century. In terms of cultural dynamics, America's role in Southeast Asia since World War II represents a continuity with Western colonialism. The economies of the Asean nations (Thailand, Singapore, Malaysia, Indonesia, and the Philippines), are particularly entwined with the United States.

Southeast Asia is at once ethnically and culturally unified and diverse. Its similarity stems in part from a time prior to the beginning of the present millenium before the area experienced the impact of India and, to a lesser degree, China. This culture developed in the most hospitable land areas—the coastal regions, river valleys, and deltas. Unlike our own country, where the culture of the American Indian was largely suppressed and rejected by European settlers, the cultures of the early peoples in Southeast Asia (e.g., the Chams in Vietnam, the Khmers in Cambodia, the Pyus in Burma, and the Malays) were integrated with later overlays from India, China, the Middle East, and the West. Our own country has been referred to as a "melting pot" of different peoples and cultures. This is true to an even greater degree of Southeast Asia. To understand Southeast Asia today, we must understand its long historical traditions which account for both its unity and diversity, and for change and development which, until today, have modified without destroying the essential characteristics of its unique cultural synthesis.

We must now discuss two major characteristics of Southeast Asian civilization at greater length. The first of these is the nature of its largely peasant, agrarian society; the second is the undisputable influence of Indian culture in the area. In both cases there are significant differences from our own country. Although agriculture has been an important part of our economy, we have not been primarily a farming or agricultural country for many decades. America is known for its industry, scientific progress, and its large cities. In Southeast Asia the converse is true. There are a few large cities, but although some of the countries in the area are beginning to industrialize, their economies and populations are still predominantly agricultural. In Southeast Asia political institutions, forms of social organization, and religion have made major shifts through the impact of outside powers both Asian and Western. Our own country, however, has been allowed to develop in relative isolation.

Rather than referring to the countries of Southeast Asia as "underdeveloped" or "developing," it is more to the point to say that their development has been different from ours. We must avoid the pitfall of judging Southeast Asia by our own values, norms, and standards. Many Americans are now questioning our precipitous industrial development and the type of life-style it has fostered. It may be that other countries, including those of Southeast Asia, have something valuable to show us.

THE NATURE OF PEASANT SOCIETY

What does it mean to say that Southeast Asia has primarily a peasant, agrarian society? The agricultural economist would emphasize that paddy or wet rice farming is the principal occupation of most people; the social anthropologist might speak of the kinship structure of peasant or rural societies; and the politician would characterize the area as needing outside capital and technical expertise to progress. While all three responses have their place, the peasant, agrarian nature of Southeast Asian society has, above all, influenced many attitudes, practices, and values held by Southeast Asian peoples.

Most Americans have grown up in a highly controlled environment. Modern machines have eased the burden of physical labor; lighting and heating systems enable us to alter the pattern of hot and cold, light and darkness; and modern modes of transportation and communication have vastly reduced conceptions of time and space. Our industrialized, highly mechanized world view greatly conditions our behavior and attitudes. Similarly, the fact that the majority of the people of Southeast Asia live in a nonindustrialized, only slightly mechanized environment conditions their attitudes and behavior. While modernity is changing life in many parts of rural Southeast Asia, these societies are still quite traditional. The forces of nature which determine the successful rice harvest are to be placated rather than controlled, and the major values of the human community are still centered about the family and religion. The most important celebrations revolve around the agricultural calendar, significant occurrences in family life such as weddings and funerals, and the major religious events of Buddhism, Islam, or Hinduism.

Roughly eighty percent of the native peoples of Southeast Asia live outside urban areas. Among them is a small proportion of relatively isolated, primitive groups who still maintain themselves by hunting and gathering wild foods rather than by cultivating crops and domesticating animals. A larger percentage of Southeast Asian people practice swidden agriculture. Small plots of jungle land are cleared and cultivated for one or two years and then left fallow while similar plots are cleared and cultivated. Tribal groups in more mountainous areas who practice this form of "slash and burn" agriculture grow millet, dry rice, maize, and opium. They tend, however, to live outside of the major peasant ethnic groups, although their way of life is threatened by modern nation-state developments.

The great majority of Southeast Asian peasantry today is engaged in paddy or wet rice farming. Wet or paddy rice farming takes place on the alluvial plains and lowland regions of Southeast Asia. The rice must be planted in flat plots which are surrounded by low earthen walls to hold the water necessary for proper growth. The most common practice is to grow the rice in a nursery plot for a period of a month to six weeks and then transplant the young rice plants into the main fields which have been cultivated and soaked with water. Farm families working together at rice transplanting time is one of the most memorable sights to the visitor in Southeast Asia. They cover the rice paddies in rows, moving rhythmically together.

Within this rural, agricultural setting, the village has traditionally been the most important social and economic unit. Economically, it is almost self-contained. A wide range of fruits, vegetables, and rice are grown and a variety of animals are raised. Furthermore, numerous handicrafts such as weaving and metalwork may be practised within the village. Traditionally, family descent has been from the mother's line rather than through the father's although this custom was more widespread in former times than it is today. One of the legacies of this matrilineal organization of society is the relatively high social status of women. For example, in rural Thailand, it is often the women who look after the

(United Nations photo/Saw Lwin)

Most of Southeast Asia's peasant farmers are involved in wet rice farming. Here, rice is planted at Ban Pra Khu village in Thailand.

economic well-being of the family and handle the family's finances.

Villages have tended to be closely knit. Marriage has taken place between members of the same village or neighboring ones. It is often the practice for the groom to live in the home of his wife's parents or, perhaps, to build a house of his own on the same compound of his new in-laws. He will help cultivate the fields of his wife's family and may, eventually, add some land of his own. Travel is still much more difficult than in our own exceptionally mobile society. Traveling shorter distances is relatively easy, however, on the many canals which mark the region's coastal plains. New roads are also being constructed in various parts of Southeast Asia, and motorized transportation is seen in most towns. Nevertheless, the oxcart and the bicycle, besides walking, are the most common modes of transporation. Electrification has broken down the isolation of many of the rural areas although it is by no means universally accessible. Sometimes the quiet of a relatively rural area is interrupted by the din of loud music amplified to the volume of some of our own rock concerts!

The standard of living in rural Southeast Asia, from our point of view, might seem only slightly above subsistence level. There is no running water, nor refrigerators or packaged foods. The typical one-or-two-room dwellings made of bamboo and palm leaves might seem interesting to visit but impossible to live in. The privacy valued by most Americans is unknown by the Southeast Asian peasant. The competitive drive which so dominates our urban, industrialized society is largely lacking in the peasant society of Southeast Asia. Even the games played by young people are mostly non-competitive in nature.

Due to the relatively small size and interdependent nature of the village, rural life tends to be typified by harmonious community relations, including a democratic election of village offices, communal plowing and land ownership, and

(United Nations photo)

The temple at Ankor is one of the finest remaining examples of Khmer architecture.

various forms of mutual aid. An entire village will participate in community celebrations such as the dedication of a new house. At a recent celebration of this nature in Northern Thailand hunters went into the jungle and shot a wild boar which they contributed to a village feast. Most of the members of the village came to pay a visit to the owner of the house to wish him well and sample some of the special treats he had had prepared. It was an occasion not unlike an Amish barnraising in our own country today.

As you might expect, the annual life pattern is governed very much by the agricultural calendar. Planting and harvest seasons are the busiest times of the year and also inspire important festival occasions. In a typical village in Burma, Thailand, and other parts of Buddhist Southeast Asia, for example, the agricultural cycle revolves around the long rice growing season from May through October. During the month of April the New Year festival occurs. It is a celebration of renewal in preparation for the coming rains and the beginning of the new agricultural year. It is a time for commemoration of deceased ancestors and for seeking the blessings of the village elders and the Buddhist priests. To the visitor, however, the most obvious forms of celebration are the water games in which nearly all young people engage. If you are in Thailand during Thai New Year, you might be startled by a stray bucket of water that is thrown by children and teen-agers on nearly all passersby.

The New Year is followed by other festivals closely associated with the agricultural calendar. In May, after the rains come and the fields are prepared for the rice, one of the most important Buddhist celebrations is held commemorating the birth, enlightenment, and death of the Lord Buddha. In July, when the rice is transplanted, rainmaking ceremonies are held, addressed to the village gods. It is a time when several of the young men of the village may be ordained as Buddhist monks. In most cases they stay in the monastery for only three months and leave the monkhood at the beginning of the harvest season in October. We generally think of the priesthood or monkhood as a lifetime vocation, and in Southeast Asia this practice is also followed. However, there is the custom of spending only a short period of time as well. Such a custom is like the Western religious practices of bar mitzvah and confirmation.

Other important village festivals are held in September when the rice has reached the critical stage in its growth, in October at the end of the rains, and in February when the rice is harvested. The harvest festival is the most important "merit-making" celebration in the village. Gifts are given to the Buddhist monks with the hope that the giver will receive meritorious rewards, leading to a better life in his next existence. Buddhists believe that upon death a person's life does not end but merely passes into another form. That form will depend in large part on the moral quality of his or her life in previous existences. Many acts performed by the villagers for the Buddhist monks or for the local Buddhist temple are done with the hope of improving their future lives.

During the harvest festival, services are held at the village temple in which one of the most popular Buddhist stories is told about a prince named Vessantara. Vessantara was the son of a king in Central India. His great delights were works of charity and self-giving. He was blessed with a loving wife and two children. And, among other treasures, he owned a white elephant which had a wonderful power of causing rain to fall. In a neighboring country where drought had caused famine, some Brahmin priests asked for his magical elephant. Vessantara gave it with delight to benefit those who were suffering. Since this act caused much dissatisfaction among his father's subjects, he was banished. Before leaving, however, he gave away seven hundred slaves, seven hundred elephants, horses, chariots, buffaloes, and all kinds of treasures. On his journey away from his homeland, he gave away his own chariot and horses to a Brahmin, and finally, even his children and his wife. As it turned out, the Brahmin priest to whom he had given the rest of his worldly possessions was the god Indra in disguise. Indra informed Vessantara that all the gods had rejoiced in the gifts he had offered and assured him that all that he had given up would be returned to him. In addition, because of his selfless nature, he would become an enlightened one (a Buddha) in his next existence.

The story of the noble Vessantara reminds the villagers of the noble virtues of self-giving and self-sacrifice and adds a strong moral dimension to the celebrations of the rice harvest. It illustrates one of the ways in which Buddhism has become a part of a festival whose origins lie in the agricultural year. In a similar manner, some of the principal Jewish festivals originated in agricultural cycles of the ancient Near East, and the Christian celebration of Christ's resurrection appropriated the rites of spring renewal.

THE INFLUENCE OF INDIA

The single most important outside cultural influence in Southeast Asia has been India. In fact, historians have referred to the region, especially the mainland peninsula, Sumatra and Java, as "the Indianized States of Southeast Asia." This influence has taken many forms. The major religions of Indianized Southeast Asia—Buddhism, Hinduism, and even Islam—have come from India. Conceptions of kinship and statecraft have often been derived from Indian models. Many arts and crafts including music and drama reflect Indian motifs. Even the mythology, folklore, literature, and language were shaped by Indian forms. Finally, Indian princes, merchants, priests, and artists individually made distinctive contributions to the development of countries in the area.

Our own country has been influenced by many European cultures. Yet, it would be difficult to say that our cultural society has been shaped by one dominant European power.

Our system of government, for example, does not imitate any particular European model and our arts are a mixture of several traditions. In religion, American culture has reflected European Protestantism but the religious freedom sought by our forefathers guaranteed that no one form of religion could exclude others. Because of our history it may be difficult for us to appreciate the decisive influence India has had in Southeast Asia beginning as early as the first or second century A.D. and lasting until the fifteenth. Yet, if we are to understand Southeast Asia, we must have some knowledge of the variety of ways in which India infused itself into the area.

The establishment of Indian influence was undoubtedly a gradual process and not a massive migration of people. It probably began with the arrival of a few merchants and adventurers who were accompanied by Brahmin priests. The three major centers from which Indian influence stemmed were probably Amaravati and Conjeeveram near modern day Madras in south India and Nalanda on the Ganges River in northern India. Indianized kingdoms arose either through intermarriage or as a result of Indian imposition on the native population. We find an example of this type of development in Funan, the forerunner of present day Kampuchea. An Indian prince named Kaudinya married the local chieftainess after subduing her people. Funan was probably the most important Indianized state in Southeast Asia from the second or third century through the eighth century A.D., and dominated much of the mainland from central Vietnam down into the Malay Peninsula.

The most interesting questions that arise from the impact of Indian culture on Southeast Asia deal with acculturation. What kind of changes took place in native attitudes, ideas, and practices as a result of Indian influence, and correspondingly, how were these Indian elements changed by the peoples of Southeast Asia? These questions not only apply to the early history of the region. Understanding the dynamics of cultural interaction between Indian and Southeast Asia is necessary if we are to be able to appreciate fully the nature of cultural interaction at later times—including the colonial and modern periods in which America has had such an important role.

Cultural interaction usually follows one of three patterns: rejection, accommodation, and transformation. The first pattern occurs when the receiving culture attempts to reject all outside influences. For example, after General Ne Win became Prime Minister of Burma in 1964, he ousted nearly all foreign groups including both private foundations and government agencies like the United States Agency for International Development (A.I.D.).

In the second pattern, the receiving culture accommodates itself to new cultural forms but with superficial rather than real change. Some of the responses to Western culture during the colonial period were of this nature. For example, even though many of the elite classes were educated in Western ways which resulted in changes of values and social and political patterns, the masses of the people were relatively untouched by Westernization. Consequently, when nationalization emerged as a potent force prior to World War II, non-Western cultural dimensions such as national dress, religion, and language became important symbols of resistence to the colonial powers. This does not mean that the colonialization of Southeast Asia was devoid of Westernization; however, even the elites of the region were not as changed as some from the West might believe.

The third type of cultural interaction is transformation. When the impact of an outside culture is very strong existing cultural forms are inevitably affected. Much of the Indian impact on Southeast Asia is of this nature. For example, there is no doubt that Indian Buddhism came to be the religion of the majority of the people in Burma, Thailand, Laos, and Kampuchea and was at times powerful in Vietnam and Indonesia. Even though earlier religious attitudes and practices continue to be important, the world view of the typical Thai or Burman today is fundamentally conditioned by Buddhist notions. Consequently, it is assumed that a Thai, a Burman, or a Laotian is a Buddhist unless identified to the contrary.

Up to this point we have generalized about three types of acculturation which might be said to take place in any country or region. By and large Indian influence in Southeast Asia was one of transformation. Yet, even though Indian culture transformed much of Southeast Asia, it did not affect all parts in the same way. It is probable that the western portions of Southeast Asia (i.e., Burma, central Thailand, Malay peninsula, Sumatra) experienced extreme accultura-tion. Successive waves of Indian influence from the second through the tenth centuries A.D. almost overwhelmed this region. Archaeological evidence points to Indian influence in art, architecture, and religion. India also strongly influenced the culture of the court, especially if it was interrelated with art and religion. The impact of India in purely secular spheres, e.g., social structure, law, and even material cul-tures, was apparently not very strong in any part of Southeast Asia. The influence of India in the western zone of Southeast Asia, therefore, was a transforming power in art, religion, and the customs of the court. It left little room for the receiving culture to respond creatively. At least in the spheres of religion, architecture, art, and court customs the pattern was almost one of transplanting Indian cultural forms.

In the eastern zone, i.e., Champa (Central and South Vietnam), Kampuchea, Java, Borneo, and Bali, the impact of Indian culture was somewhat less strong. Archaeological evidence indicates that while Indian culture in the areas of art, architecture, religion, and court customs was pervasive in the area, it underwent greater change than in western Southeast Asia. Consequently, Austro-Asiatic cultural ele-ments persisted in some form or other. Furthermore, unique cultural forms developed as a result of the interaction between Indian and Austro-Asiatic culture.

Examples of this type of dynamic cultural interaction are the famous temples of Borobudur in Java and Angkor Wat in Kampuchea. These temples are among the wonders of the world and rank with the pyramids or the greatest cathedrals of Europe in their magnificence. Borobudur and Angkor Wat emerged from a synthesis of Austro-Asiatic and Indian cultural forms. One of the principal characteristics of the Austro-Asiatic culture was the existence of large stone mounds or megaliths. These megaliths were associated with burial practices and the spirits of powerful rulers. In Southeast Asia this particular practice emerged with the Indian association of mountains and deities to form a massive, mountain-like temple symbolizing the power of the ruler as a god-king or a divine being.

The great temple of Borobudur was built during the eighth and ninth centuries A.D., during the reign of the Sailendras, a powerful dynasty in Java and the Malay peninsula of the mainland. The body of the structure consists of six square terraces becoming smaller as they ascend. The temple was inspired by a form of Buddhism popular in northern India at this time known as the Mahayana or Great (Maha) Vehicle (Yana). It probably depicts the progress or path of devoted Buddhists as they strive to tread their way from the world of everyday things (the lowest terrace) to the highest point of self-realization (the highest terrace). The structure also has an important meaning related to the Sailendra rulers. It symbolized a mountain from which the king ruled his world. In short, it was a cosmic mountain or a mountain of a divine king whose power was made even greater by his identification with the holy Buddhas of Mahayana Buddhism.

The temple of Angkor in present day Cambodia is even more awe-inspiring than Borobudur. As Henri Mouhot, the French explorer who rediscovered Angkor Wat in the nineteenth century, and others observed, this architectural work perhaps has not, and perhaps never has had, or ever will have, its equal on the face of the globe. This monument to the gods and to the rulers of the mighty Khmer Empire is characterized by a majesty, might, dominion, power, harmony, and beauty which have been hardly diminished by the eight hundred years of its existence. The temple was built in the twelfth century when the Khmer Empire was exceptionally strong on the Southeast Asian mainland. It was originally dedicated to the Indian god Vishnu but, as with the temple of Borobudur, the king (Suryavarman II) was identified with the god. Thus, Angkor Wat was not simply a temple in honor of the gods. More importantly, it was a living memorial to the ruler of the ancient Cambodian empire.

The temple is massive—a perfect square 220 yards long with its topmost tower rising 220 feet in the air. Angkor Wat is ten times the size of the famous cathedral of Canterbury in England. It was built with slave labor and with great expense to the kingdom. It rose from the flat plains surrounding it as a mountain of the god-king symbolizing the presence of the deity and the power of the ruler. While the original inspiration for the temple—like Borobudur—must have come from India, the Austro-Asiatic culture of Southeast Asia transformed the meaning of the structure. It was not simply a dwelling place for the gods. Rather, it was the abode of the king who was divine. This conception of the god-king or the divine ruler has been very important in the history of Southeast Asia. Not only was it significant in ancient times but in modern times as well. We shall return to this subject when we examine political developments in the post-colonial period.

The culture of Southeast Asia was transformed by India. In some cases Indian cultural forms were simply transplanted into the region, took root, and flowered. In others, as in the examples of Borobudur and Angkor Wat, the substance was decisively changed and given a meaning it did not have in India itself. Just as Southeast Asia cannot be properly understood without some knowledge of its earliest peoples and their cultures, so it cannot be truly appreciated without an acknowledgment of the crucial role India played in its early development. This process of cultural rejection, accommodation, and transformation has been a continual part of the history of Southeast Asia. No culture is completely static although cultural change takes place at very different rates in differing times and places. We are mistaken, however, if we view as unique our own time of rapid social and cultural change. Just as we hesitate to make generalizations about our own country today because they might be outdated tomorrow, so we should hesitate to make generalizations about Southeast Asia—about what it was or what it is.

THE GREATNESS OF SOUTHEAST ASIA

How great is a civilization? What is the measure of its greatness? How great is America? In the 1950s many of us probably would have replied, "America is great." We saw our country as the bastion of freedom and democracy, defending Europe from the onslaught of Soviet Communism and South Korea from Maoist Communism. We had not yet begun to face up to the problems of urban blight, racism, environmental devastation, and an oft-criticized foreign policy in Southeast Asia and Latin America—problems which preoccupy many of us today. Our national identity in the Eisenhower years was generally confident and self-assured. During the past decades, however, that picture of America has gradually tarnished. Some historians, for example, have begun to point to our long tradition of racism which has extended not only to black Americans but to various minorities in this country including, in particular, the American Indian. Some political and social scientists are growing increasingly critical of certain facets of our government and economic system. Nearly everyone is concerned about having a place to live and work in reasonable safety from crime and pollution. In an age of questioning, we should examine ourselves not only negatively, but positively. We should reflect on our present in the light of an honest understanding of our past—the good points and the bad.

Most of Southeast Asia has recently emerged from a long period of Western influence and domination. This emergence has led, in some cases, to a reappreciation of its historical traditions, especially the great periods in its history. As Americans trying to understand Southeast Asians, we need to recognize the great periods of their history. We err if we see countries like Burma, Kampuchea, and Thailand only in terms of our own cultural and historical perspectives. We need to make the effort to see them as they see themselves, not as underdeveloped but as developing countries with oftentimes grand moments. These grand moments are very important in a consideration of the question we asked earlier, "What is the measure of a civilization's greatness?" Certainly, one answer might be, "A civilization is as great as its greatest moment." We shall now look briefly at a few of the great moments in the history of Southeast Asia.

The splendor of Angkor Wat was mentioned earlier. It was built during one of the great moments in the history of Cambodia. During the reign of Suryavarman II and Jaya-varman VII in the twelfth and thirteenth centuries, the Khmer Empire reached the height of its power. Under the latter ruler, Cambodian territory extended from the capitol of modern-day Laos in the north to the Malay Peninsula in the south, and from the east coast of Vietnam to the frontiers of Burma. It was a flourishing period of Cambodian art and architecture as the building of Angkor Wat and other great temples illustrates. A strong literary movement was carried on, much of it in Sanskrit, the classical language of ancient India. The influence of Cambodia at this time is seen not only in its massive building programs or the extent of its boundaries. If we examine the twelfth- and thirteenth-century remains of the capitol of Thailand, we see the strong influence of Cambodian architectural forms. From historical sources we know that the Thai conception of kingship and structure of political authority was influenced by Cambodia also.

Turning briefly to Burma, we find that the country was united for the first time in the eleventh century under King Anawrahta (1044-1077) who ruled from the capitol of Pagan in northern Burma. He apparently established his sway over much of what is now northern Thailand and appropriated the form of Buddhism known as the Theravada (Teachings of the Elders) which had reached its height in Sri Lanka (Ceylon). In all probability this form of Buddhism was adopted through the influence of a people conquered by King Anawrahta in southern Burma, a people known as the Mons. The Mons were among the earliest people to settle in the Southeast Asian peninsula and were also the first Indianized people in Burma. They adopted Theravada Buddhism through the influence of India and acted as one of the principal agents for its spread not only in Burma but Thailand as well. Indeed, Theravada Buddhism became the principal, official religion of Burma, Thailand, Laos, and Cambodia.

The visitor to Pagan is struck by the close relationship that must have existed between Buddhism and the state. Temple and monastery ruins cover acres of land and the most impressive temples were built by King Anawrahta and his successors. Just as in Cambodia both Buddhism and Hinduism lent sanctity and authority to the king. He, in turn, was the protector of religion. It was a reciprocal relationship in which religion and the state enforced one another. Such a complementary pattern is, of course, not unique to Asia. Similar patterns emerged in Europe as well. And, despite the tradition of the separation of church and state in America, organized religion has often served to support the ideals of patriotism and national unity. To understand Southeast Asia properly we must recognize the important supportive relationship that has existed between religion and the state.

Two of the great moments in the history of Indonesia are represented by the Sumatran-based Srivijaya kingdom and the Sailendra kingdom on Java. We mentioned the Sailendras in connection with the great monument of Borobudur. Srivijaya rule was even more important because it held sway over the Straits of Malacca, parts of the Malay Peninsula, and parts of Java as well as Sumatra for over five hundred years. It was the major commercial power in Southeast Asia during this time because of its commanding position on the sea route between India and China. A Chinese Buddhist pilgrim who visited Srivijaya in the late seventh century noted in his diary that over thirty-five Persian merchant ships had arrived during his stay. The principal ports of Srivijaya, which included Malacca, Achin, Batavia, Penang, and Singapore, must have been highly cosmopolitan centers with traders and merchants from India, China, various parts of the Middle East, and even Europe. The strategic location of Srivijaya and the important role played by Arabs in the trade between East and West led to the establishment of Islam in this region.

Southeast Asia, if measured in terms of its great historical periods, its magnificent monuments, and its cultural depths, is indeed great. In terms of art and architecture, conceptions of kingship and law, philosophy and religion, and the scope of commercial activity, Southeast Asia compares favorably with Europe. And America, at the time of the grand moments of Southeast Asian history, had not yet been discovered by our European forefathers.

2

CHALLENGES TO POLITICAL AND SOCIAL ORDER

How do you view your life? Do you see a consistent "you" in time and space without much change? Or do you see yourself as continually changing, developing, maturing? In fact, as you examine your own past, you might see your life in stages. There may be plateaus of no great dramatic change but other stages where you reached a real turning point. The histories of nations and of cultures follow similar paths. In the case of Southeast Asia, for example, the impact of Indian culture produced a real turning point in the histories of several countries. These changes did not take place overnight. Nevertheless, Indian influences moved Southeast Asia in a direction it probably would not have taken otherwise.

Not only India, however, transformed the culture of Southeast Asia. Prior to the appearance of the West on the scene, parts of Southeast Asia were subjected to the influence of Chinese and Islamic cultures. In this chapter our particular interest will be the presence of Western powers in Southeast Asia but only after some attention has been paid to the influence of China and Islam.

CHINA AND SOUTHEAST ASIA

The location of Southeast Asia places it between the spheres of Indian and Chinese power. Yet India had the greatest impact on the region. From time to time China attempted to raise its political umbrella over most of the area, but with only nominal success. Culturally, the role of China in Southeast Asia bears no comparison to that of India. A list of China's influences would include: the ceramics of Thailand in the thirteenth and fourteenth centuries, the decorative arts of the early Srivajaya kingdom in Sumatra, the trade of the region during much of its history, and the claims of political suzerainty China attempted to make during periods of her greatest internal unity. One aspect of the legacy of this varying Chinese presence in the area is a sizable Chinese minority in almost all parts of Southeast Asia, much of it brought by the British and the Dutch. In some instances—Thailand, for example—the Chinese have been reasonably well-integrated into the life of the country. There they play a very important role economically. In other countries, such as the Philippines and Indonesia, the Chinese have not been assimilated as well. With the ascendance of General Suharto and subsequent ouster of Sukarno in Indonesia, the Chinese suffered greatly. Even in Thailand where Thai and Chinese relations have been much better, the dissolution of parliament and the assumption of complete control by a military clique in the fall of 1971, were partially justified on the grounds of the threat posed by the large Chinese population in the country.

The greatest influence of China, however, has been in Vietnam. Indeed, North Vietnam (or Nam Viet as it was called) was incorporated into China in the first century B.C. North Vietnam remained a part of China until the Vietnamese successfully revolted in the tenth century. However, this long period of Chinese influence left an indelible stamp. It can be seen in the language and literature, art and architecture, Chinese Buddhism, Confucianism and Taoism, and the development of a characteristically Chinese educated elite or mandarin system. Vietnam continued to acknowledge the suzerainty of Peking, but it was never really completely dominated by China again. This relationship between Vietnam and China, which entails a deep cultural dependence and yet a strong desire for political independence, is an important aspect of Vietnam's attitude toward China today. In addition, the homeland of Vietnam has traditionally been the North; the Vietnamese only gradually pushed toward the South. The kingdom of Champa which had existed for hundreds of years to the south of Vietnam was only decisively defeated in the latter part of the fifteenth century. Indeed, many former political leaders of South Vietnam today originally came from the North.

ISLAM IN SOUTHEAST ASIA

Islamic influence in Southeast Asia began with the Persian traders who plied the ports of Srivajaya; however, Islam did not become a potent force until the fourteenth and fifteenth centuries. At that time it was spread primarily by Islamic merchants from north India—another legacy of Indian influence in Southeast Asia. The first strong center of Islam was Malacca on the Malay Peninsula. It became one of the most important ports and trading centers in the area. Gradually, Islam spread to the coastal areas of Sumatra and Java as local rulers converted to Islam in the hope of gaining wealth and commercial success in their trading ventures. Eventually, before the middle of the sixteenth century, the once powerful Hindu kingdom of Majapahit fell before a coalition of Malayan and Javanese Muslim states. Islam spread throughout the Indonesian Islands and even further north to the Philippines where it was finally stopped by the intrusion of the Spanish. Only in Bali, one of the most beautiful and exotic islands in the world, did Hindu culture remain strong. The remnants of pre-Muslim cultures in Bali make it one of the most interesting places to visit in the Indonesian islands.

From its very beginning in the Near East in the seventh century, Islam has been important as a religious movement and also as a political force. Islamic authority was established in North Africa, the Middle East, and even made inroads into Europe. It crossed the Indus River into India where the differences between Islamic and Hindu cultures ultimately contributed to the creation of Pakistan, a separate Islamic state. In Southeast Asia, Islam introduced elements of Arabic culture reflected in language, literature, and the arts. Islam became a powerful political force as it had in other parts of the world. Islam took its firmest hold in Malaya and Indonesia and claimed religious loyalty and political allegiance. In neither of these two countries did a religious state emerge as it did in Pakistan; however, Muslim political parties did develop. In Indonesia, for example, one of the first groups to rally the cause of national independence against the Dutch was Sarekat Islam, the Islamic Association. And, after its demise, other Muslim political parties followed in its wake. Furthermore, the current resurgence of militant Islamic movements in the Middle East can be seen on a smaller scale and in less dramatic form in Indonesia and Malaysia.

Prior to the West's entry into the Southeast Asian orbit, Indian influence had nearly transformed pre-existing cultures in the western part and had decisively influenced the culture of the eastern part. The impact of China had been felt most profoundly in Vietnam; and that Islamic-Arabic influence had been confined largely to the trunk of the mainland peninsula and the islands of Southeast Asia. Much as we react to outside influences in terms of rejection, accommodation, and transformation, Southeast Asia responded to India, China, and Islam. Islam took Indonesia by storm but the Balinese refused to capitulate to its power. China tried to assert its authority over much of Southeast Asia, and many rulers accommodated themselves to its nominal suzerainty with little practical effect. India offered the Sailendras and Khmers a view of the king which provided the basis for new forms of political organization.

These are a few of the examples of the cultural synthesis—

WESTERN COLONIZATION
IN SOUTHEAST ASIA

Increasing Western domination in the late 1800s caused disruption of indigenous cultural patterns. World War II sparked a resurgence of national identities in Southeast Asia.

in its unity and variety—that emerged when Portuguese and Spanish merchants and missionaries first established themselves in Southeast Asia in the sixteenth century. A similar pattern of rejection, accommodation, and transformation can be applied to the interaction of the West with Southeast Asia. It will be helpful to keep this pattern in mind as we begin this consideration of the colonial period.

COLONIALISM AND ITS IMPACT

The Southeast Asia that the Western powers encountered in the sixteenth century was a cultural crossroads for Austro-Asiatic peoples, Indians, Chinese, and even Arabs. To this mixture, the Portuguese and Spanish, the British, Dutch and French, and finally the Americans have now been added. The age of the Western powers in Southeast Asia covers roughly four hundred years from the middle of the sixteenth century to the present. It can be conveniently divided into three main periods: from the arrival of the Portuguese and Spanish in Malacca and the Philippines, respectively, in the mid-sixteenth century until the early nineteenth century; from the mid-nineteenth century when the Dutch dominated Indonesia, the British Burma, and the French Indochina to the conclusion of World War II; and from the period of national independence following the War to the present in which the dominant Western power is the United States.

The first period is characterized primarily by Western commercial and trading enterprises such as the Dutch, British, and French East Indian trading companies, and relatively small settlements of Europeans in the region. Second to commercial interests were religious aims, especially on the part of the Catholic powers: Portugal, Spain, and France. In general, however, Western influence was not particularly strong, and the issues of prime importance were largely Asian rather than European. Europeans did not radically challenge indigenous ways of life. New groups of

Southeast Asian leaders emerged; and in the eighteenth and nineteenth centuries there were wars, dynastic upheavals, population displacements, and struggles for power and wealth among bureaucrats, landowners, and nobility. New states arose and disappeared, and there was little preparation on the part of the Southeast Asian leaders themselves for the onslaught of Western power to follow—especially in Burma, Indochina, and Indonesia. Leaders in Thailand and Malay proved to be more astute in their attitudes toward the West. The Philippines—with a strong Spanish presence—is somewhat of an exception to the pattern followed in other parts of Southeast Asia.

The second period of Western presence in Southeast Asia is marked by the increasing dominance of the West. By 1870, much of the territory of Southeast Asia had passed formally into the hands of European interests. Close links, especially economic, developed between the mother countries and their colonies which reduced interregional contact. The nature of colonial administrations and the responses of particular Southeast Asian countries to them varied greatly. As a result this period is a very complex one. It is impossible, within the scope of so brief a book, to do justice to the complexity of this period. Generally speaking, this period of colonial history in Southeast Asia was much more disruptive of indigenous life patterns whether economic, social, or political. In later chapters, we shall note examples from separate countries for certain trends. The trends will help us in our understanding of the entire region.

The third period, marked by strong nationalistic aspirations, focuses on the era of World War II. The Japanese role in Southeast Asia, in countries like Indonesia, for example, was extremely important in the development of nationalistic interests. The Japanese both wittingly and unwittingly were one of the most important catalysts in the rise of the nation-state in Southeast Asia following the war. But it would be a mistake to see Asian nationalism as simply a product of

World War II. As early as the turn of the century, nationalistic movements of one kind or another were emerging in Burma, Indonesia, and elsewhere in the region.

Western dominance is, as we know, a story not yet ended. The British in Burma and Malaya, the French in Indochina, and the Dutch in Indonesia have ceased to control these countries, although their presence is still felt in many ways. Direct political involvement on the part of the United States changed decisively with the end of our involvement in the Vietnam War in 1978. However, we continue to exert a powerful economic and political influence. American oil companies are extremely interested in having an Indonesia favorable to the West, the Dole Company now has a major interest in Thailand's pineapple plantations, Southeast Asia has become an important source of cheap labor for our microelectronics firms, and our government supports a strong alliance among the ASEAN nations. Southeast Asia is entering a new age in which there is a greater possibility of a regional community where both East and West cooperate as equal partners.

Before looking more specifically at some of the developments in Southeast Asian countries under colonial regimes, it should be emphasized that the colonial picture is not all negative. Today we are apt to condemn "colonial imperialism" as a period of exploitation of weaker and less developed countries by powerful Western European nations. There was, to be sure, a great deal of economic exploitation. The economies of Southeast Asian colonies were basically geared to the needs of Western markets. Yet the Western presence in Southeast Asia also produced beneficial results. In Malaya, for example, the British helped to bring about a closer cooperation between small states than had previously been possible. A Malayan Sultan, when asked if he wanted to be free from the British, replied, "Freedom? What do you think we pay the British for?"

What happened during the hundred years of Western

dominance in Southeast Asia? What did the Europeans think of their presence in the area? How did the peoples of Southeast Asia respond to them? Francis Garnier, a French administrator in Cochinchina (South Vietnam) wrote in 1861:

> Let us give the most complete liberty to the election of the chiefs; let us increase their influence and privileges, let us make them the born natural defenders of the population. When this foundation of the structure is thus carefully preserved and respected, the Vietnamese will accept very quickly ... French administrators replacing the greedy mandarins at the head of the state. At the same time, the arrival of European commerce, the opening up of markets will increase the general wealth a hundredfold and will topple the latest prejudices. When the works have been executed, when the means of communication will have been established, the measures taken for the benefit of public hygiene will appear to them to be worthy of admiration and gratitude.[2]

In Indonesia, a rural rebellion in West Java in 1926 led to a commission of inquiry set up by the colonial government the following year. Its report included the following: "This time it was so-called communists, another time it will be extreme nationalists or others who attempt the same thing. The urge for freedom which stirs the best among these people ... is not to be checked by any contrived system of preventive or repressive measures, but perhaps the excesses to which it gives rise in these regions may be prevented by always and unreservedly granting the population a voice in administrative affairs corresponding to its own development. As the population's share in the settlement of its own interests becomes larger, counter-forces may be developed which will turn against any organizations which jeopardize authority."[3]

Of course, the peoples of Southeast Asia responded to the

colonial experience not as the ruler but the ruled. In some cases there was bitter condemnation of the colonial regime. In others, we see the pathos of the loss of cultural identification through extensive Western influence. Nguyen-Thai-Hoc, founder of the Vietnamese Nationalist Party, wrote in a letter from a French prison after an anti-French uprising in 1930

> [During the uprising] the French Indochinese government burned and destroyed their houses. They sent French troops to occupy their villages and stole their rice to divide it among the soldiers. Not just members of my party have been suffering from this injustice . . . but also many simple peasants, interested only in their daily work in the rice fields, living miserable lives like buffaloes and horses, have been compromised in this reprisal. At the present time, in various areas there are tens of thousands of men, women and children, persons of all ages, who have been massacred. They died either of hunger or exposure because the French Indochinese government burned their homes. I beseech you in tears to redress this injustice which otherwise will annihilate my people, which will stain French honor, and which will belittle all human values.[4]

On June 20, 1935, Sutan Sjahrir, one of the prominent leaders of the Indonesian nationalist movement and Prime Minister of Indonesia following World War II, wrote in a letter to his wife

> Am I perhaps estranged from my people? Why am I vexed by the things that fill their lives, and to which they are so attached? Why are the things that contain beauty for them and arouse their gentler emotions only senseless and displeasing for me? . . . We intellectuals here are much closer to Europe or America than we are to . . . the primitive Islamic culture of Java and Sumatra. Which is our basis: the West, or the rudiments of feudal culture that are still to be found in our Eastern

society? . . . for our spiritual needs we are in general dependent on the West, not only scientifically but culturally.[5]

In general terms, it can be said that the West had diverted much of the Southeast Asian life from its own native course and forced it into entirely new channels. These new channels included food production, drastic population changes including rapid growth and the creation of minority problems, qualitative changes in social organization, and a major alteration of political structures. We shall briefly examine each of these problems.

The population of Southeast Asia grew from approximately twenty-six million in 1830 to 123 million in 1940, and today is close to four hundred million. This rapid growth was, in large part, a result of colonialism. Western authority in the area served to reduce self-destructive, internecine warfare, new crops were introduced and new lands brought under cultivation, and Western means of health care reduced mortality rates. In mainland Southeast Asia the delta areas developed rapidly, making the region a major rice exporter. In some cases the economy came to be dominated by a major crop. In Java, for example, sugar cane production increased tenfold from the 1860s to the turn of the century. Agricultural specialization was usually dictated by the economic interests of the Western powers and sometimes resulted in hardship to the native peoples. Expansion of agricultural lands served the positive purpose of breaking down relative geographic and cultural isolation. On the negative side, it produced major population shifts and accompanying problems. Java, for example, had been brought to the point of dangerous overcrowding by the mid-twentieth century.

Colonial policy was governed primarily by economic considerations dictated by the needs of the mother country. Economic development often did not benefit native populations and in fact brought about severe social problems.

Internal population shifts resulted in dislocation from traditional social settings. A more serious problem was the importation and resettlement of large numbers of outside laborers in Southeast Asian countries. In most cases they were either Indians or Chinese. These minorities, on the one hand, added to the population problem in already overcrowded areas. On the other, they tended to be more favored than the native peoples themselves because these outsiders were brought into the area by the colonial powers for specific purposes. As one observer remarked, the native population became "aliens in their own lands."

One of the major social changes brought about by colonialism was the superior place assumed by the Western ruling elite. Unlike the Indians who colonized Funan, Champa, and the early kingdoms of Southeast Asia, the Westerner made little attempt to become a part of Asian culture. He brought with him Britain, France, Holland, and America. If you were to visit Singapore today, for example, you would be struck by the impressive buildings constructed under the British colonial administration. However, in nearly every respect they are British and not Malayan. Or, if you were to visit Bangkok and a friend took you to the Royal Bangkok Sportsclub, you would learn that the impressive facilities were, in fact, the Royal British Sportsclub prior to World War II. It was a place where the European elite could come to swim, play tennis, and watch horse-racing. The exclusiveness and implied superiority of the European elites became a source of deep resentment.

Not only were the traditional elites of Southeast Asian societies partially displaced by their Western rulers; they also took a back seat to other Asians brought into their countries, especially in the growing urban areas. Consequently, a new kind of "caste" system developed with Western, Indian, and Chinese minorities living in relatively isolated enclaves and being in the most favored social, political, and economic positions. This pattern of an exclusivistic, ethnic pluralism stands in decided contrast to the precolonial period where ethnic groups were better integrated. The racial, ethnic, and cultural segregation which characterized colonial Southeast Asia was a consequence of the policies of the Western countries involved. Americans in Southeast Asia have followed much the same pattern. A visitor to Bangkok, especially in the 1970s, would note that Americans are concentrated in an exclusive suburb of the city. In addition, too often Americans in Southeast Asia act with cultural arrogance and superiority.

To leave the impression that colonialism meant a repression of all native groups would be incorrect, however. In Vietnam and the Philippines, for example, a new kind of bourgeoisie arose who shared in the wealth of the new agrarian economies. Also, many Burmans, Thais, Cambodians, Vietnamese, and Indonesians were educated in the West and returned to their countries to assume places of leadership within the colonial structures. In some cases these leaders were members of the traditional aristocracy. In others, they were from lower social classes who, because of their abilities, were able to change their social status. In challenging traditional social hierarchies and patron-client relationships colonialism provided for a social mobility that might not have developed otherwise, providing rewards not only for status but for ability. The development of a relatively broad-based intelligentsia eventually was to work against the colonial powers. It created a manpower capable of providing leadership for the revolutionary movements working to overthrow the colonial regimes.

New ruling classes, the creation of an agricultural proletariat based on the expansion of production, and the emergence of a bourgeoisie and intelligentsia brought about the important social changes affecting traditional political structures. We will now examine the impact of colonialism on these structures.

Traditionally, the "state" was conceived in terms of

cosmological sanction. For example, in our discussion of the Sailendras and Khmers in Chapter 1 we noted that their rulers were thought of as "god-kings" who ruled from a "holy mountain" like Borobudur or Angkor Wat. They were looked upon either as divine or as holy persons responsible for the well-being of the state within the framework of a natural order. Consequently, the traditional state was dynastic rather than territorial and was usually rather limited in territory although boundaries varied greatly. By way of contrast, as historians have observed, the colonial state was equipped with an unprecedented physical power. Because its primary function was to exercise power as supreme policing agent placed atop the colonial society, it drained its subjects of real political existence. It is important for us to keep in mind that even though colonial regiments wielded immense amounts of power and were respected for it, they never enjoyed the legitimating sactions of tradition and religion. By way of contrast we have seen how precolonial settlers in Southeast Asia (e.g., Indians) oftentimes brought with them the sanctions of tradition and religion which served to engender their rule with an even more superior authority.

Colonial political authority may be divided into two main types: direct and indirect. Indirect rule which maintained at least the appearance of the native status quo usually cushioned the impact of Western modernization. Laos and Cambodia under France, the Unfederated Malay States under Britain, and some of the lesser Indonesian principalities under Dutch rule are examples of indirect colonial rule. In some instances indirect rule even served to increase the prestige of the ruler. In the case of Cambodia, for example, the absolute, semi-divine nature of the monarchy was given encouragement; and in Indonesia a few monarchal states were actually created in the nineteenth century. The maintenance of the traditional ruling class served to lessen the strong degree of political alienation which developed in countries governed by direct rule.

Southeast Asian countries under direct rule in the nineteenth century included Lower Burma, Annam or Central Vietnam, and the economically important areas of Indonesia such as Java. These areas experienced the full impact of modernization and, in some cases, Westernization. (It is important to note that modernization and Westernization do not necessarily mean the same thing.) Native political systems and religious establishments suffered the most. In Burma, for instance, the monarchy was destroyed in 1886, as was the Vietnamese monarchy at Hue at about the same time. The religious establishments which had generally been closely intertwined with the monarchial political structure also declined. In Burma, enforcement of the Buddhist monks' discipline was generally lax, and morale was at a low ebb. The British government followed a policy either of noninterference or of encouraging the work of Christian missionaries. In neither case was there the kind of support that Burmese Buddhism had grown accustomed to in precolonial times. In directly ruled colonies, therefore, there was a strong alienation from the modern political order on the part of two of the most important orders of society—the ruling aristocracy and organized religion. It was this sense of alienation which lay at the heart of the desire for independence.

Colonial rule sowed the seeds of its own destruction. Aimed primarily at the economic well-being of European countries, it was not sufficiently sensitive to the social and political realities of the colonies. Resentments grew progressively stronger. In Southeast Asia these resentments bubbled into movements for independence in Vietnam, Burma, Indonesia, and Malaya. It is to the development of national independence that we will now turn our attention.

INDEPENDENCE AND NATIONALISM

We in the United States have a certain common history with the desire of Southeast Asian nations for freedom and independence. After all, our nation was born out of a struggle for independence from Great Britain. Many of the political slogans of the early nationalist movement in Southeast Asia are similar to those slogans of our own revolutionary period ranging from "no taxation without representation" to "give me liberty or give me death." This common idiom with Southeast Asian independence movements made our role in the Vietnam War a peculiar one. While there is no doubt that it was a policy partially determined by our fear of international communism (the "domino theory"), in some respects it was a continuation of an indirect form of colonialism. Thus, to many Southeast Asians, we appear to be a nation which grew out of the rejection of colonialism only to become a colonial power ourselves.

This movement toward independence from the suzerainty of the West might be seen basically as a movement toward a new self-identity. There is, of course, a redefinition of one's self or one's group in any period of revolution or of rapid social and political change. For example, you, at one time or another, have probably found yourself in a demanding situation as a result of which you saw yourself in a different light. You took on a new self-identity. This is similar to what happened in the drive of Southeast Asian countries toward national independence. In part, this new self-definition was a consequence of the new political boundaries that had been drawn by the West's occupation of their territory. It was also a product of Western ideology from which Southeast Asian leaders learned the concept of the modern nation-state. This concept involved a more universal sense of identity which transcended dynastic and communal loyalties. Earlier foci of loyalty such as religion (e.g., Buddhism, Islam) were used to strengthen loyalty to the concept of the nation-state. In Burma, Indonesia, and Vietnam anticolonial movements were often originated in religious organizations.

Southeast Asian nationalism as we know it today is a result of the colonial period. One face of it is the strong, negative reaction of Southeast Asian leaders to the yoke of Western power. The other face of Asian nationalism is shaped by Western models of political structures and processes and even the concept of the nation-state itself. Nationalism in Southeast Asia is, therefore, a contradiction. One observer has expressed the contradiction this way:

> ... a great part of the inner dynamics of nationalism in Asia must result from this profound contradiction within nations that derive from an ancient Asian past and yet have been brought to national awareness not only by the Western impact but ... by the revolutionary appeal of their own native Westernizers.[6]

Asian nationalism is the result of the interaction of two different political and social systems: modern-Western and traditional-Southeast Asian.

Independence movements in Southeast Asia began as early as the latter part of the nineteenth century. The first well-organized anticolonial movement was in the Philippines where social evolution and Westernization had progressed beyond the rest of Southeast Asia. José Rizal became one of the Philippines' most celebrated national heroes when he was executed by the Spanish in 1896, two years before Commodore Dewey destroyed the Spanish fleet in Manila Bay. Under the Americans the Filipino Nationalist Party ran the legislative system until full independence was granted in 1946.

In several other countries of Southeast Asia, independence movements centered around religious groups. In Indonesia, for example, it was the Sarekat Islam, organized in 1912; in Burma, it was the Young Men's Buddhist Association, founded in 1908. These groups served as a staging ground for more secularly based movements which developed later; however, in the early stages of anticolonialism they provided reformist and revolutionary leaders with a locus of support. Even though anticolonial movements were frequently

associated with traditional groups such as Islam in Indonesia, Buddhism in Burma, or the Confucian Mandarins in
Vietnam, the leadership did not harken back to a precolonial
past. In most cases the leaders of these movements were
either educated in the West or in Western methods at
universities in Asia. For the most part they were highly
trained intellectuals and professionals. In the Philippines,
Quezon and Osmena were both lawyers with experience in
the West. Luang Pradit in Thailand was a lawyer trained in
Paris. In Burma, Aung San was a law student from Rangoon
University (a Western-oriented university) and Baw Mau
studied at Cambridge. In Indonesia, Sukarno was an engineer
by training and Sutan Sjahrir an intellectual with an intimate
acquaintance with the West. Hence, one of the contradic-
tions of Asian nationalism is that the leadership did not come
from the traditional cultural reservoirs of Southeast Asian
countries. On the contrary, those Southeast Asian people
who were most directly influenced by the West were in the
forefront of the movements for independence. For the most
part they did not want to reject the West out of hand. Rather,
they wanted to adapt the dynamism that had revolutionized
the West to the traditions of their own countries.

Several models—both Western and Asian—were important to these early leaders. The American and French
revolutions and the political philosophies of Marx and Lenin
were important. Ho Chi Minh, for example, Vietnam's
greatest leader since the colonial period, was a committed
Marxist as early as 1920. Several Asian models provided
special inspiration. The Vietnamese were particularly influenced by China—Sun Yat Sen, the Kuomintang party,
and finally the Chinese Communists, especially Mao.
Gandhi and the Indian National Congress were also models
to be studied and followed. Yet the West, which had
subjected Southeast Asia to colonial dependence, was still
the primary inspiration for reformist and revolutionary
philosophies and methods. The Western colonial rulers had,

on the one hand, made the new leaders of Southeast Asia more aware of their own native, non-Western cultural traditions; on the other, they provided them with the philosophies and the mechanisms for going about the job of fashioning new nation-states through the transformation of their own cultural traditions using Western ideas and methods. Many historical events hastened the independence of Southeast Asian countries, particularly the Japanese occupation of much of the region during World War II. Nevertheless, the heart of colonialism—economic interests determined in Europe—spelled Western colonialism's doom.

The fight to gain independence was not an easy one. The fledgling anticolonial movements gradually gained momentum in the early twentieth century. World War I and the Communist revolution in Russia in 1917 sparked a movement toward a more revolutionary form of nationalism. In Indonesia the PKI or Indonesian Communist Party broke with the Sarekat Islam and succeeded in developing a large peasant following. This success coupled with terrorist activities led to the repression of the Party in the late 1920s. The nationalist cause was then picked up by the PNI or Indonesian Nationalist Party led by Sukarno, one of the most important figures in the entire history of the independence movement in Southeast Asia. He and other PNI leaders were exiled to remote islands and were released only with the Japanese invasion in 1942. In Burma, the nationalist cause gradually expanded from its base in the Young Men's Buddhist Association to a group called the General Council of Burmese Associations. Yet, even the General Council was governed by politically active Buddhist monks. In the 1930s, more secularly oriented organizations such as the Thakins and the A.F.P.F.L. (Anti-Fascist Peoples Freedom League) emerged. It was in the latter organization that contemporary leaders like U Nu and General Ne Win came to prominence as important political figures. U Nu, in particular, ranks with Sukarno as one of the great national leaders of this period (see Chapter IV).

The cause of independence in Indonesia and Burma was carried on primarily by radical nationalist leaders. Yet, in Vietnam, it was Ho Chi Minh, a committed communist, who led the field. He organized the Indochinese Communist Party and worked in various ways for the overthrow of the French in the 1920s and 30s. The nationalist cause was also furthered by a noncommunist, socialist party known as the VNQDD or Vietnam Nationalist Party which received support from the Chinese Kuomintang. It proved to be less successful, however, than Ho Chi Minh's political fortunes. Ho spent nearly thirty years exiled from his homeland, and it was only in 1944 that he was allowed to return to Vietnam and direct the fight for independence personally. He was acknowledged to be the most popular national leader in the entire country and was admired by Vietnamese throughout Vietnam. Ho had early connections with the United States. He visited this country before World War I, and he also received arms and ammunition from the United States Office of Strategic Services in the 1940s. We later reversed that policy and supported the French position against Ho's nationalist movement.

The battle for Vietnam in which the United States invested so many lives and billions of dollars, in many respects began in 1946 when the French refused to acknowledge the aspirations of the Vietminh, Ho's resistence movement and one of the strongest national political organizations in the country. The United States' financial stake in the war was considerable; by 1953 we were paying eighty percent of France's military expenditures in Indochina. Unfortunately, like the French, the United States government saw the war largely in military terms rather than as essentially a problem of creating a government capable of winning mass support.

The time in which we live is one of rapid social and political change. Political change in Southeast Asia has meant the creation of independent nation-states. The Philippines received their nationhood in 1946; the British relinquished Burma in 1948; independence was granted to Indonesia by the Dutch in 1949; the French were defeated at Dien Bien Phu in 1954; the Federation of Malaya was formed in 1957; and the Malaysian Federation (Malaya plus Singapore, Sabah and Sarawak) was formed in 1963. The emergence of the nation-state is a movement toward a new self-definition brought about by the colonial period. The traditional, dynastically oriented political structure was decisively challenged by the modern Western notion of the nation-state. Yet, no single political pattern has emerged from the post-World War II period when most of Southeast Asia won its independence from Western colonial powers. In general, four types of political regimes have emerged into the 1980s: military-authoritarian, civilian-authoritarian, communist-authoritarian, and democratic.

Powerful military factions are in control of the governments of Burma, Indonesia, and Thailand. General Ne Win has controlled Burma since 1958. Efforts to establish an effective Burmese socialism independent of the communist superpowers have been frustrated by serious internal conflict with sizeable minorities in northern Burma, and a go-it-your-own economic policy of gradual agricultural and industrial development without much capital assistance from the West. Mineral-rich Indonesia, one of the most populous countries in the world, has been governed by General Suharto since he took over in 1966 from Sukarno, Indonesia's great leader of national independence. Suharto's domestic and foreign policies have been decidedly pro-West. He has established a mass national party to consolidate his own power base in the military, has sought extensive aid from the United States and other Western powers, and has encouraged a wide variety of projects aimed at national development. Thailand's recent political history has been somewhat more checkered than Burma's or Indonesia's, and there was an "experiment with

(United Nations photo)

President Sukarno of Indonesia was one of the most prominent leaders of the nationalist movements which took hold among the former colonies.

democracy" between 1973 and 1976. The country, however, has been essentially controlled by various military
groups since the end of World War II even though there are
national elections (as recent as April 1983). Thailand is also
the only Southeast Asian country with a reigning monarch.
The country was an absolute monarchy until 1932 and since
that time the king has continued to be an important symbol of
national unity.

The political configuration of Southeast Asia is diverse, as
the chart on the following pages shows.

Southeast Asian governments have been dominated by
authoritarian regimes of one kind or another. Only Singapore,
Malaysia, and the Philippines have experienced long periods
of democratic rule. Singapore, with the highest standard of
living of any Southeast Asian nation and one of the greatest
economic success stories in recent years, has been run with a
firm hand by its able Prime Minister Lee Kuan Yew and the
People's Action Party (PAP) since independence in 1965.
Malaysia's 1982 parliamentary elections made Datuk Seri
Dr. Mahathir Mohammad the country's fourth prime minister.
His election was especially noteworthy because he is the first
Malaysian prime minister who is not from the traditional
Malay aristocracy or educated as a lawyer in England.
Mahathir also received strong support from progressive
Muslim political leaders commited to making Islam relevant
to modern Malaysia. In the Philippines, a showcase for
democracy since its independence in 1946, President
Ferdinand Marcos declared martial law in 1972. While most
Filipinos saw this as a necessary step toward political and
economic stability, the continued suspension of civil and
political liberties have been considered an attempt to per-
petuate the personal power of the president. Although local
elections were held in 1980 the Marcos regime is considered
authoritarian. He has suppressed political opposition, and
centralized power in the hands of close family associates.

SOUTHEAST ASIA: POLITICAL SYSTEMS

Southeast Asian political systems have been dominated by authoritarian forms of government of one type or another.

	Population (million)	Population Growth Rate %/year	Life Expectancy years	Per Capita GNP $ U.S. 1980	Urban Population %
Burma	33.5	2.2	54	170	25
Cambodia	n.a.	n.a.	45	n.a.	10.3
Indonesia	152	2.3	53	450	18
Laos	3.5	2.2	42	90	11
Malaysia	13.5	2.0	66	1,520	41.2
Philippines	48	2.7	60	720	34
Singapore	2.5	1.2	71	4,340	84
Thailand	46	2.1	61	680	18
Vietnam	56	2.4	63	170	20 (approx.)
Japan (for comparison)	115	1.0	75	8,890	68.1

These figures are derived from United Nations and U.S. State Department sources.

Electric Energy produced: KWH per capita 1980	Political System 1980	Predominant Religion	Ethnic Groups (% of total population)
42	Military Authoritarian	Theravada Buddhist	Burmese, 75; Indians, 9; Karens, Shans, Kachins, 7; Chinese, 5
n.a.	Communist Authoritarian	Theravada Buddhist	Khmers, 85; Annamese, Laos, Chinese, 15
96	Military Authoritarian	Muslim	Javanese, 45; Sundanese, 17; Madurese, 10; Others, 28
253	Communist Authoritarian	Theravada Buddhist; Animist	Laos, 48; Phoutheung, 25; Others, 27
725	Democracy	Muslim Buddhist	Malays, 47; Chinese, 34; Indians, 9
382	Civilian Authoritarian	Catholic	Filipino, 95; Chinese, 2; Others, 2
3,000	Controlled Democracy	Buddhist Taoist Confucianist	Chinese, 79; Malays, 12; Indians, 9
330	Military Authoritarian	Theravada Buddhist	Thais, 85; Karens, Khmers, 3; Malay, 3; Chinese, 9
69	Communist Authoritarian	Mahayana Buddhist	Annamese, 88; Khmers, 4; Chinese, 6; Others, 2
4,435	Democracy		

They are intended for comparison purposes.

His strongest rival, Senator Benito Aquino, was assassinated in 1983 upon returning from self-imposed exile.

The authoritarian regimes have been either a military or communist type. We are perhaps most familiar with the communist countries, the Indochina states of Vietnam, Cambodia, and Laos. We know of them because of the Vietnam War, the presence of many Indochinese refugees in this country, and the fact that the policies of the United States, China, and the Soviet Union continue to be influential in the future of these countries. With support from the Soviet Union, Vietnam essentially occupies Kampuchea where it is fighting a protracted war with a Cambodian coalition of Prince Sihanouk, Son Sann, and the Khmer Rouge (The Coalition Government of Democratic Kampuchea). This coalition represents both traditional Cambodian cultural and religious values in Prince Sihanouk as well as the radical communist forces of Pol Pot, the leader of the Khmer Rouge, which attempted to destroy the economic, political, and social infrastructures of Cambodia at the end of the Vietnam War. Laos is also dominated by Vietnam, but the Laotian government has taken a somewhat more cooperative attitude toward its noncommunist Asian neighbors.

The political uncertainty of Southeast Asia is not unique to that area of the world. Student demonstrations in the United States in the late 1960s and early 1970s, reflected not only disagreement with America's foreign policy in Southeast Asia, but a conviction that the American democratic system was not living up to its ideals. Can significant political change take place without destroying existing mechanisms of government? Does stability inevitably mean stagnation or can stability and change go together? What is the relationship between historical traditions and the dynamic of change? Questions such as these are relevant to our own political situation as well as to that of Southeast Asia.

LOCUS OF CHANGE: THE CITY

We have noted that nearly eighty percent of Southeast Asia is rural. Even so, nearly every Southeast Asian country has a major urban center which is the focus of power and the locus of change. These include Manila in the Philippines, Rangoon in Burma, Bangkok in Thailand, Singapore, and Djakarta in Indonesia. In several respects these urban centers, which became important centers of commerce and trade during the colonial period, provide laboratories for examining the problems resulting from the challenges of modernization and Westernization. Looking at the cities is like viewing the challenges to political and social order through a magnifying glass.

Just as the notion of the modern nation-state is a Western invention, so the city in Southeast Asia is a result of Western colonialism. As one scholar put it, "The large city . . . is a foreign innovation, possessing a high proportion of . . . (non-native) inhabitants, serving mainly foreign interests, and tacked onto a rural background."[7] With the exception of Bangkok which was built by Thai kings, the major cities were built by foreign interests primarily as commercial centers. Only later did they become administrative centers as well. Because the cities were the most important loci of develop-ment during the colonial period, they tended to be the areas where the conflict between tradition and change focused. They were the centers where many young Southeast Asians were educated and came into firsthand contact with foreign intellectual and political influences.

The cities, furthermore, were places where traditional social structures were frequently undermined. Attracted by the lure of jobs and higher standards of living, peasants flowed into the cities from the countryside. Subject to new social and economic pressures many of the old customs associated with the village were destroyed. As the population increased, overcrowding occurred and slums were created.

Because cities are the most important centers of power, they attract young, educated Southeast Asians who want to be there rather than in towns and villages. The cities are where the opportunities are and where much is going on. While there is a rural urban gap in this country, it does not compare to that in Southeast Asia. In the United States there are many cities of different sizes, and our development has been such that the rural-urban gap has been largely bridged. In Southeast Asia, however, the difference is so acute that it is difficult to entice trained professionals to leave the city.

Let us examine the Southeast Asian city by looking at Bangkok, the capitol of Thailand. The city was founded in 1782, less than twenty years after the Thai capitol of Ayuthia had been destroyed by the Burmese. Since it was the only major Southeast Asian city not built by foreign interests, parts of it still retain a fascinating "oriental" charm although there has been phenomenal change within the past two decades. Today greater Bangkok is a city of over four million. It is the rail center for the rest of the country, has the only major port, and the only international airport. Until recently the only universities were in Bangkok although new regional universities have now been built in the north, northeast, and south. Bangkok also houses the national museum, the national library, and the national school of fine arts which is attempting to preserve traditional Thai music and dance. Because of its central location in Southeast Asia, Bangkok is the headquarters for several international organizations including the United Nations Economic Commission for Asia and the Far East. Bangkok is the commercial center of Thailand and most industrial development that has taken place is near the city. In sum, Bangkok is clearly the hub of the country's transportation, education, cultural arts, commerce, and industry, and the seat of national government.

In recent years Bangkok has changed radically. Old canals and halting trolleys have made way for four-lane super-highways. Modern, air-conditioned hotels are everywhere, and the noise of building construction shatters the air. Cars crowd the streets, and the stores are filled with American and Japanese luxury items. As one of the tourist capitols of Southeast Asia, it attracts many Western visitors. Many are Americans and in the recent past a large percentage of them were either military personnel or their dependents. The international school in Bangkok whose enrollment is largely composed of Americans has over fifteen hundred students.

Bangkok has become a hothouse in which the tensions between Western culture and Southeast Asian culture meet head-on. The role of Americans and other Westerners in Bangkok is similar to that of the French in Saigon prior to World War II. In particular, the difference in the standard of living between Americans and many of the Thais around them is startling. Yet it is not simply the difference in living standards. It is a difference in cultural styles. As one hears American rock music and sees young Thais imitating American styles of dress and behavior, one wonders what types of changes are taking place. Are the educated and privileged Thais who are most exposed to American influence being deeply changed, or are the effects largely external? If you have foreign students in your school, you might ask them to talk about the way in which their experience in this country has affected the way they think about their own country. Has their American exposure made them critical of their own country's customs, mores, and ways of doing things or has it given them a new appreciation of their native culture?

3

CULTURAL REVOLUTION

A Thai teacher in a Bangkok high school who had earned a university degree in the United States once talked about her frustrations as a teacher at her school. The basis of her unhappiness was the fact that she had spent four years in this country and was finding it very difficult to readjust to her own culture. She had been so influenced by American ways of doing things, American attitudes toward people, and so conditioned by her school environment in the United States that she had become uncomfortable in her own culture. This teacher is not really an exception. Thousands of Asians have been educated in this country and Europe. Many of them have become so oriented to Western ways that they have no desire to return to their home countries. When they do return to their homelands, they often feel like fish out of water. The impact of the West has been so strong that it has caused them to reject many of their cultural values. This kind of cultural disassociation has also affected Southeast Asians who have not left their own countries but who have been direct beneficiaries of the colonial system. That is, they were educated in European language schools and were brought into colonial administrations.

The reaction of Southeast Asians to "Westernization" has not always resulted in the rejection of the native culture. On the contrary, sometimes the opposite response occurred. Some of the most important leaders in anticolonial movements were either educated in the West or studied in European language schools in their native countries. They were directly exposed to the Western values of individualism, the idea of the nation-state, rational-scientific methods, and the philosophies of political and social revolutionaries like Marx and Lenin. In turn, they integrated what they learned into their own cultural and value systems in such a way that they were led to revolt against their Western leaders. It has been this group of Asian reformers and revolutionaries who have been responsible for bringing about another cultural transformation in Southeast Asia. True, they have rejected much of what they learned about Western culture. Yet, the ideas and methods of the West provided them with the means for revitalizing their own cultural traditions. In this chapter we shall examine the impact of Western education in the cultural revolution associated with the colonial and post-colonial periods, the transformation of traditional Southeast Asian worldviews rooted in Buddhism and Islam, and, finally, the challenge to traditional values and social customs in such developments as tourism and industrialization.

EDUCATION

Education has provided one of the most important vehicles for cultural change in Southeast Asia. It has caused some to reject many aspects of their own culture; it has given others perspectives which have led to cultural transformation. Both responses figure prominently in our understanding of Southeast Asia today.

The importance of education in the development of a nation was clearly recognized by Thomas Jefferson, the founder of the University of Virginia, and other authors of the American Constitution. The system of land-grant colleges in America is an example of the interconnection between education and national development. Finally, colleges and universities in America today are reassessing their role in relationship to national priorities and needs as diverse as nuclear research and financial aid for draft non-registrants. Not only in this country but in Southeast Asia, education has been important in national development. Indeed, it has probably been one of the single most significant avenues for cultural change in the colonial and post-colonial periods.

Education played a variety of roles during the colonial period. One of the most important was to train a group of people who would be capable of filling subordinate administrative roles in colonial administrations. As the British Inspector of Schools put it on the occasion of the creation of Malay College in 1905,

> [We must produce] a vigorous and intelligent race of young men who will be in touch with modern progress but not out of touch with old traditions; who will be liberally educated but not educated out of sympathy with their own families and people; who will be manly and not effeminate, strong-minded but not strong-willed, acknowledging a duty to others instead of being a law unto themselves and who will be fit to do something in the world instead of settling down into fops, spendthrifts, or drones.[8]

Malay College succeeded in this aim. In the past it was the principal means by which Malays joined the ranks of the Malay Administrative Service and the Malay Civil Service. Indeed, one authority claimed that Malay College served to set the tone for the moderate nationalism that has characterized Malaysia.

Malay College did more than prepare Malayans for administrative and civil services, however. It socialized its students into an upper-class English cultural environment. The school was like a typical English boarding school complete with playing fields, headmasters, prefects, and all the other aristocratic trappings. The medium of instruction was English, and it produced men who were more at home on the cricket field and at high tea than in the villages of Malaya. Here is what one Malayan graduate of the College had to say after a hard-fought rugby match against the team from an opposing college:

Wasn't our Headmaster a very proud man after that?
The names of the team will ever remain fresh in my
memory. The team never broke up until the time came
for us to leave College. . . . Those were glorious and
unforgettable days in College when we learned hard
and played hard, inspired by great teachers who gave
us, among other things, all that was best of the
traditions of English education.[9]

Until the advent of the Western powers, education in most
of Southeast Asia had been in the hands of organized religion
or controlled by such traditional methods as the Confucian
examination system in Vietnam. In Burma and Thailand, for
example, education was carried on in the Buddhist monasteries and temples and included training primarily in Buddhist
doctrine and ethics as well as in the rudiments of reading and
writing. The coming of the West meant the development of
secular education not only in the form of elite English
language schools like Malay College but vernacular schools
as well. Subjects taught reached beyond the usual disciplines
of the monastery or other traditional subjects, thereby
opening up new intellectual horizons. But secular education
also had the effect of undermining traditional values and
social commitments. A study of Burmese civil servants, for
example, showed a causal relationship between crime and
education. Secular, Westernized education had failed to
integrate moral values with training in skills as had been true
in the traditional form of education. As a consequence, so-
called "modern" education had, in one sense, served to
undermine the moral community characteristic of traditional
Burmese society. Furthermore, the transplanted British
system of education did not serve to meet the most pressing
public needs for better medicine, improved agriculture, and
more reliable roads in Burma. While the education provided
by British schools in Burma may have made good civil
servants in the British colonial administration, it tended to

undermine the traditional moral values and did not train the Burmese in much-needed technical and vocational skills. The present Burmese Revolutionary Government of General Ne Win has sought to emphasize science and technology, although the greatest reforms have been on the ideological level. If education in Burma is to serve the best interests of the country, technical achievement and ideological indoctrination should be integrated into the traditional Buddhist value system of that country.

Education, then, serves cultural revolution best when it does not close its eyes either to past traditions or to modern innovations. To ignore change is to imitate the ostrich with its head in the sand; however, to be a slave to the whims of new fashions is to follow the "will of the wisp." In Indonesia such a balance is suggested by a reform movement which gradually transformed the traditional Islamic education based on memorization of the Koran and repetition of the Five Duties of the devout Muslim. A modern, graded, partly secularized, formally organized school was introduced into the established Islamic traditional education. While this change came in part from the influence of Dutch government and Christian missionary schools, its main source of inspiration was a reform movement within Arabian Islam which reached Indonesia in the eighteenth and nineteenth centuries. This development is important in Muslim education in Indonesia because it attempted to preserve religious and traditional cultural values within a modernized and rationalized school.

Given the importance of education at times of significant cultural change we would do well to reflect on our own educational system. What kinds of needs is it meeting? What sorts of values is it teaching? Does our public educational system integrate the ideals and values of the public good with a scientific training relevant to a world in the midst of rapid social, political, and economic change? In sum, how well does our education relate to both the value and technological revolution in which we now find ourselves? Such questions apply to our own situation as well as to Southeast Asia despite the significant contextual differences.

RELIGION

One of Thailand's leading intellectuals, Kru Krit Pramote, was once asked, "What are the most important cohesive forces in the nation?" His immediate reply was, "The King and our Buddhist religion." Religion has been regarded as one of the most important integrative forces in society. Religion is often the basis for a society's sense of itself as a united moral community. It provides means for meeting life's most devastating crises, e.g., suffering, death, and a common idiom for explaining some of our most deeply felt needs and desires. While some Westerners have come to see religion as the "opium of the masses" (Karl Marx), or as an illusion based on psychological needs (Sigmund Freud), in most traditional societies of Southeast Asia, religion still plays an important role on the individual and societal levels. It is worth noting, for example, that in Kampuchea the Vietnamese have attempted to legitimate their role in the country by restoring a modicum of institutional Buddhism which had been eliminated by the radical policies of Pol Pot in the late 1970s.

We have already seen that some of the earliest anticolonial movements in Southeast Asia had origins in Buddhism and Islam. Buddhist monks played an active political role in the Vietnam conflict, and were also influential in the recent political history of Burma. Throughout the history of most Southeast Asian countries there has been an intimate connection between religion and the community.

Because religion is so closely associated with the cultural traditions of a country, the posture of organized religion vis à vis change is extremely important. How does religion react when caught in the throes of change? Does it retreat, follow the latest fads, or does it make a serious effort to transform its cultural and social context, and find that it is transformed in the process? These questions apply to religion in America as well as in Southeast Asia. Some churches in this country have adopted a posture in which the social and political problems we face have nothing to do with religion. At the other extreme, some religious groups seem to have become so identified with the values of our secularized culture that they have ceased to be anything more than a glorified Rotary Club. Both reactions are inadequate. Religion performs its most important function in a changing society when it avoids the extremes of cultural rejection on the one hand, or total cultural identification on the other. In this country and in Southeast Asia, religion has an important role to play in cultural transformation.

Several religious traditions that have been important in the history of Southeast Asia are indigenous forms of animism, i.e., the worship, Hinduism, Buddhism, Islam, and Christianity. The last has been particularly important in the Philippines where Spanish-imported Roman Catholicism has been the dominant religion. In Vietnam and other large overseas Chinese communities the values of Confucianism are particularly important. Recently in Singapore, one of the most highly developed urban societies in Southeast Asia, the government called for a return to the Confucian values of filial piety and respect for authority.

In mainland Southeast Asia, Buddhism, in particular, has been of great significance, and in Malaysia and Indonesia, Islam is the dominant religion. In this section we shall examine the nature of the classical Buddhist and Islamic traditions and then look at how these traditions have responded to the cultural revolution taking place around them.

At the outset we should observe that many different patterns have emerged or are emerging. In some cases the traditional religious worldviews and value systems and their

(United Nations photo)

Religion is one of the most cohesive elements in a culturally diverse region. Here, two Buddhist monks wait for a train at the Bankok railroad station.

accompanying institutional structures, have been drastically eroded. Kampuchea provides one example of this kind of development where the radical Marxist policy under Pol Pot attempted to destroy the Buddhist underpinnings of that society. In Malaysia and Indonesia, on the other hand, we find a resurgence of relatively conservative Islamic groups striving to preserve traditional Islamic values in social and political spheres. In the Philippines, moreover, Catholic Bishops are beginning to speak out against some of the more repressive policies of President Ferdinand Marcos in a manner similar to political criticisms made by their counterparts in Latin America.

Buddhism arose in northern India in the sixth century B.C. It was founded by a man with the family name of Gautama and the given name of Siddhartha. He, like Jesus, came to be given a title—the Buddha or the Enlightened One. That is, one who has discovered the truth about the nature of things.

According to tradition, Siddhartha was born as the son of the ruler of the Sakyas, a small clan living in an area near the present border of India and Nepal. The Buddhist legends speak of his miraculous birth. (There are some interesting parallels between the stories of the birth of Jesus in the New Testament and those of the future Buddha in the scriptures of Buddhism.) Being the son of a king, Siddhartha was given everything his heart desired according to the customs of royalty. He was surrounded with every conceivable luxury so that he would not be exposed to any of the minor or major "ills that flesh is err to." One day, however, while riding in his royal chariot, he came across three successive sights that startled him from his complacent life. He chanced upon an elderly person, a diseased person, and a corpse. Never having encountered old age, suffering, or death before, he was startled into a deep reflection about the nature of life. Finally, he encountered a wandering hermit. His charioteer explained that here was a man who had set himself to see if he could not find more in life than old age, suffering, and death.

Siddhartha decided to embark on a similar quest. He turned away from the riches he had known to the attainment of a higher end which the Buddhists call Nirvana. At this point, when confronted with the question of what he sought, the future Buddha thought, "When the fire of lust is extinct, that is Nirvana; when the fires of hatred and infatuation are extinct, that is Nirvana; when pride, false belief, and all other passions and torments are extinct, that is Nirvana. . . . Nirvana is what I am looking for. It behooves me this very day to quit the household life, and to retire from the world in quest of Nirvana."

With this resolution Siddhartha spent the next six years investigating various teachings and practices which might provide some insight into a higher life than one ending only in suffering and death. Finally, having found all other methods inadequate, he launched one of his own. He adopted a Middle Path which avoided the extremes of hedonism and asceticism and eventually found the end he sought. Fundamentally, his insight was that the life we take to be unchanging and permanent is changing and impermanent. The objects of our desires which we hope will quench our thirsts are vain illusions like the desert mirage. No worldly objects or goals can bring about an end to the suffering of life. This end comes when we seek not to possess life but to understand its changing nature. With that understanding we are released from all egocentric desires which—in the Buddhist understanding—are at the heart of all human suffering. If we can overcome the ego, then we can find the peace and freedom of Nirvana.

Buddhism, then, places a person on a higher way to a higher goal. It developed as a tradition centered in the monastery, a withdrawn community of people dedicated to the pursuit of Nirvana. It also developed certain practices—notably meditation—which aimed at the achievement of the same "enlightenment" the Buddha reached. There is nothing extraordinary about meditation practice in the Buddhist view. It does, however, demand a special effort for it is difficult to practice during day-to-day activities. For this reason a monastic environment was important.

Even though we think of monks and monasteries when we picture Buddhism in Southeast Asia, this religion was also important for ordinary people. Buddhism evolved a code of ethics very reminiscent of the Ten Commandments. Since Buddhists accept life as a continuous stream of existences rather than one lifetime marked by birth and death, the practice of good deeds in order to ensure a better life in a future existence is a very important part of the lay Buddhist's religious life. Westerners often find this idea of rebirth difficult to understand. Our orientation is so much toward this life, toward its improvement, or toward its pleasure that we think of life only in terms of the present. Such a strong orientation toward the present is in large part a product of our industrialized, urbanized, scientifically minded society. Yet our present problems of environment, population, and war may give us a renewed appreciation for the past and future rather than simply the present time.

Even though the Buddhist tradition in Southeast Asia focused on the monastery, it became imbedded in the cultural traditions of the countries where it took root. Buddhism became a determinative factor in the Asian personal and social consciousness. It contributed to attitudes of life and death; it inspired the architecture and splendor of the ancient capitols of Pagan in Burma, Sukhothai in Thailand, and Angkor Thom in Cambodia. Buddhism formulated ideals of governance according to the pattern of a righteous, ideal ruler and assumed responsibility for protecting the continuity of life at times of crises such as death. It influenced other great religious philosophies such as Hinduism and Taoism; and it continues to be the major social institution outside the family in much of Southeast Asia. Today, the traditional role of Buddhism is being challenged by Western political and social theories, religious values, modern technology, and the many tensions accompanying modern life. Buddhism in Southeast Asia is faced with a crisis. Can it continue to function as the touchstone of the cultures of Burma, Thailand, and much of Indochina; or will it be surpassed by a more secular world view? The answer to this question depends in large part on the kinds of responses Buddhism is able to make to the present cultural revolution.

One response is a renewed political activity on the part of Buddhist monks and laypersons. We have seen that the early anticolonial movement in Burma grew out of the Young Men's Buddhist Association (YMBA). In Vietnam, Buddhists played an important role in bringing down the Diem regime in 1963, and in that country some Buddhist monks used self-immolation to protest the war. While the political activity of Buddhist monks may seem contradictory to the almost other-worldly teachings of Buddhism, historically Buddhism has always been closely tied to the state. One could argue, therefore, that the contemporary reassertion of Buddhism into the political scene is a restoration of the sociopolitical importance of Buddhism in precolonial days. It is true that the methods used today are quite different from those of five and six hundred years ago.

There are other ways in which Buddhist monks are becoming involved in the sociopolitical arena. In Thailand, one of the Buddhist universities has begun a program to train monks in the procedures of community development. They are learning how to assist in the development of community leadership, to offer appropriate advice on rural economic problems and to function as liaisons between the people and government officials. This last role points out the trusted position held by the Buddhist monk in rural Southeast Asia. He is one of the most highly regarded members of any village. Buddhist university officials insist that the new training the Buddhist monks are receiving is nothing but an attempt to restore the place held by the monk in an earlier day when he taught in the village and advised on many matters now handled by government and secular officials.

Buddhism is embarking on new methods of education for monks and laymen alike. Buddhist universities in Thailand which used to teach subjects exclusively related to religion are now modernizing their curriculums so that their catalogs look very much like those of secular universities. Subjects are offered in the social sciences and humanities, and there are even courses on effective communication and speech. Buddhist laity are being taught by methods that remind us of our own system of sabbath day school. Such changes in educational patterns are important if Buddhism is going to retain the respect of the educated elite. In the recent past, secular education has far outstripped religious education for both monk and layman. As a result, respect for the Buddhist clergy has tended to decline in the cities among the educated classes.

Another response to the cultural revolution in which Buddhism is enmeshed is a renewed emphasis on social ethics or the responsibility of Buddhists in the world. While this theme has been the focus of Judaism and Christianity, it has not been emphasized in Southeast Asian Buddhism. Indeed, in some respects the pursuit of Nirvana seems to have a touch of otherworldliness. Partially in response to the influence of Christianity, Buddhists are stressing the importance of the individual's role in the world. Indeed, popular sermons on this subject sound very much like sermons in this country which stress the need for people to look after those who are less fortunate than themselves. One prominent Theravada Buddhist, the Venerable Walpola Rahula, has said:

> Buddhism aims at creating a society where the ruinous struggle for power is renounced; where calm and peace prevail away from conquest and defeat; where the persecution of the innocent is vehemently denounced; where one who conquers oneself is more respected than those who conquer millions by military and economic

warfare; where hatred is conquered by kindness, and evil by goodness; where enmity, jealousy, ill-will, and greed do not infect men's minds; where compassion is the driving force of action; where all, including the least of living things, are treated with fairness, consideration, and love; where life in peace and harmony, in a world of material contentment, is directed towards the highest and noblest aim, the realization of Ultimate Truth, Nirvana.[10]

In addition to adaptive responses to cultural, social, and political challenges, some Buddhists seem more interested in trying to protect traditional institutional forms from the effects of modern, secular developments. The Buddhist monastery can no longer claim to be the center of community activity in many towns in contemporary Thailand, for example. And traditional formulations of such life problems as why people suffer, and how that suffering can be overcome may no longer be satisfying to the educated populace of Laos or even Burma. Those who would attempt to hold on to the "old ways" simply because that is the way things have always been done face the inevitable consequence of becoming outdated and irrelevant. To be sure, many traditional Buddhist teachings, such as the essential interdependence of all forms of life, or the inevitable moral consequence of all our actions, and of the virtues of simplicity and non-attachment to material goods, seem to be eternally valid. But their application must be shaped by current needs. For example, in the economic sphere we find Southeast Asian Buddhists who are setting up rural development schemes appropriate to the limited technology and wealth of the Southeast Asian peasant rather than Western models which often presuppose an unrealistic level of material prosperity. These schemes embody Buddhist values without harkening back to a preindustrial or predevelopment point of time. Only with creative change can Buddhism continue to provide the sort of leadership necessary to help its cultural societies through the present revolutionary period. It is not enough simply to assert old ways and old values. There must be an interaction with new attitudes and ways of doing things.

This challenge confronts Christianity and Judaism in the West as well. Religion's role is to transform society, but in the process of this transformation, religion is also changed. It cannot remain static and unchanging. Perhaps this is our own personal challenge as well. How can we respond to change, growth, and development without losing our sense of balance, stumbling, and falling down? If we are to survive, we must be equal to the challenge.

Islam arrived on the historical scene later than Buddhism. Reflecting an indebtedness to both Jewish and Christian backgrounds, its founder, Mohammed, taught in the area of Mecca and Medina (now modern-day Syria) in the seventh century A.D. Unlike Southeast Asian Buddhism but like its Semitic predecessors, Islam is monotheistic, i.e., it affirms the worship of one God. Of all the theistic religions, in fact, Islam is the most uncompromising in its insistence on the holiness and transcendence of God as reflected in the universal Muslim confession of faith, "There is no God but God (Allah) and Mohammed is his prophet." This God is revealed in nature and, more particularly, through his prophets, especially Mohammed. Muslims believe that religion is not separated from the rest of life. The principle of the separation of church and state is therefore foreign to Islam. It is the task of every Muslim to follow God's will in everything. It is often said that Islam is built on the principle of unity which has three aspects: the unity of God; the unity of truth; and the unity of human life.

Islam emphasizes the importance of social relationships, not only the family and the community, but the state and the universal brotherhood of Islam, as well. The Islamic tradition of social ethics is, perhaps, even stronger than in Buddhism. These are codified in an orthodox tradition of sacred scripture, the *Q'uran* (or Koran), overseen by a group of experts in Muslim law. Southeast Asian Muslims, like Muslims everywhere, respect the Five Pillars of Islam: the Confession of Faith in one God and his prophet, Mohammed; the five daily prayers facing Mecca, the holy center; fasting during the lunar month of Ramadan; pilgrimage to Mecca; and the payment of a religious tax.

Although Islam has these universal aspects, it also absorbed different cultural elements in various parts of the world to which it spread, e.g., India, Southeast Asia, and Africa. In Indonesia, for example, scholars point to three-types of religion: a village religion which represents a synthesis of animism, Hinduism, and Islam; a kind of Javanese mysticism inherited from the Hindu-Javanese court of the Majapahit kingdom of precolonial times; and, a purer form of Islam concentrated in the business classes, a tradition stemming from the introduction of Islam to Indonesia as part of the great trade expansion from the Middle East and Europe. Although there is evidence of Islam in Sumatra as early as the thirteenth century, the first Islamic kingdom in Indonesia was on Java and dated from the first quarter of the sixteenth century. Today, Indonesia is the largest Islamic nation in the world. The 1973 census showed Muslims constituting eighty-seven percent of a population of 120 million.

Because of the Islamic view of the unity of all human life and the close identification of religion and the state, it has played an important role in Indonesia and Malaysia as they have developed into modern nation-states. In Indonesia the first Indonesian nationalist movement was the Islamic Association (Sarekat Islam) which stemmed from the Muslim Traders Association founded in 1911. Another important Indonesia Islamic movement was the Muhammadijah founded in 1912 with the purpose of promoting Muslim religious education and religious life in the face of secular education established by the Dutch. It was an adaptive or reformist movement in that it sought to cooperate with the Dutch

government and advocated study of Western secular subjects as well as Islamic history, doctrine, and practice. It
sought a compromise between more conservative Indonesian
Muslims who insisted on the observance of old traditions,
and the secularists who had been won over by Western
technical and scientific ways of thought. The Muhammadijah
maintains that Muslims should continue to have a firm
identification with traditional ritual and beliefs of Islam, but
it is ready to deal with problems of modernization.

The revival of Islam in the Middle East has its parallel in
Southeast Asia as well. In Indonesia there has been a
resurgence of religious building and attendance at religious
activities. In particular, there has been an increasing involvement of youth and there are now Mosque Youth
Associations flourishing throughout the country, especially
in large cities. A wide range of social and religious activities
are offered by these associations, from sport and self-defense
arts to music and academic discussions. As in the Middle
East, this revival must be seen, at least in part, as an assertion
of a national cultural identity over the secular West.

Over the past ten years Islam has been both the agent and
symbol of many rapid social changes affecting Malaysia. It
has become a source of identity for various elements in
Malaysian society, distinguishing Malays from non-Malays,
and has helped to legitimate various new elites emerging in
Malaysian society. In an earlier day, universities were dominated by English-speaking elites; however, as Malay-medium
students have come to predominate on university campuses
they have not only asserted the dominance of Malay as a
language but as a race and religion (i.e., Islam) over non-
Malay and non-Muslim minorities. Across the entire nation
associations are developing with the intent to incorporate
religion into the daily lives of the membership. Although the
Islamic content of these groups is problematic, all share in
the spirit of Islamic revival. There are even three such
associations on the national level. One is the Islamic Youth

Movement (ABIM), whose aim is to "re-Islamize" the Malays and extend the scope of religion beyond mere ritual acts. The ABIM has established its own schools, produces a voluminous amount of literature, has developed various social services, and has considerable political influence.

Religion in Southeast Asia has historically played an important role in forming the cultural, political, and social identities of its followers. In the modern period it continues to play a significant role in the nation-building process. In some cases, religion seems to have moved very much to the periphery, as in Kampuchea. In other instances, however, it continues to underlie the beliefs and value systems of the people in Thailand and Burma, for example. In still other countries, like Malaysia, expressions of religious revival have come to the fore in political, economic, and social spheres.

VALUES, MORES, AND SOCIAL CUSTOMS

The societies of Southeast Asia are still largely traditional. They are still dominated by a strong family structure, with age-old patterns of prescribed behavior between young and old, male and female. In our own competitive society, the family structure is now being challenged, and modes of behavior between ages and sexes are not clearly delineated. When Americans enter into a traditional society, they are aware of real differences. For example, we are unfamiliar with the kind of deference to age that still typifies most Southeast Asian societies, or with the kinds of restrictions surrounding relationships between males and females—especially among young people. (Movements like the Women's Liberation are largely foreign to Southeast Asia.)

Precisely because of these differences, our presence challenges the traditional values, mores, and social customs of Southeast Asia. Unknowingly, we become agents of a cultural revolution on this level. During the late 1950s, a young American taught English in a Thai high school. The classrooms were very dirty. The teacher thought that the situation ought to be rectified, and he organized a work crew consisting of himself and a group of students and teachers. It was his idea to thoroughly sweep and scrub down one of the classroom buildings in order to set an example that might then be followed by others. During the clean-up, he noticed the students and teachers he had recruited were reticent. It was only afterwards that he realized the two mistakes he had made. In the first place, he had asked both students and teachers to do a task of manual labor that was beneath their status, and, in the second place, he had placed students and teachers on the same level working at the same task. To Americans, for whom class consciousness is relatively unimportant, his attempt to clean up the dirty classrooms might be taken for granted. To the Thais, however, he had either committed a social error or, in his own way, had staged a minor cultural revolution.

Regardless of our intentions, when we enter into Southeast Asian society, we cannot help but affect certain values, mores, and social customs. Sometimes, perhaps, we affect them negatively. At other times, we may have a more positive influence. It is incorrect to look at the interaction of Americans and Southeast Asians and make the judgment that all of our cultural values are bad and those of the Southeast Asians all good or vice versa. Cultural values are relative to a particular time and a particular place. Our goal should be to try to understand the values, mores, and social customs of Southeast Asians with the hope that we can interact with them more intelligently and sensitively.

Since the end of the Vietnam War, thousands of Cambodians, Laotians, Vietnamese, and Hmong have settled in cities and towns through America. Many have adjusted to urban life, often living on the fringes of blighted ghetto areas. They must acquire sufficient English to be able to communicate, find employment, and learn about American mores and customs. Our major news magazines have reported on the high rate of suicide among Laotian men, of Vietnamese fishermen being attacked by the Ku Klux Klan in Texas, of Hmong tribeswomen building cooking fires in the middle of tenement living rooms as though they were village huts, and of many incidences of gambling and alcohol abuse. Other stories have told of successes against nearly overwhelming odds, of exceptional academic performances by hardworking Southeast Asian children, and of the development of cooperative associations for mutual assistance against an often frightening environment. Few of us can really understand the difficulty that many Southeast Asian refugees have adjusting to American culture. In the deepest sense, it is a challenge to their identity as Laotians, Cambodians, and Vietnamese. Their often rural, peasant lifestyle hardly fits into the mold of our American city life. The values of a tightly-knit extended family infused with tradition and religious beliefs are often at odds with our own values and lifestyles.

Yet the plight of Southeast Asian refugees in America is echoed in the cities of Southeast Asia, especially in Manila, Singapore, Kuala Lumphur (Malaysia), Djakarta (Indonesia), and Bangkok. The rural poor of Thailand or the Philippines, for example, flock to Bangkok or Manila looking for relief from poverty. They seek jobs in construction; however, many turn to prostitution. In Penang (Malaysia) or Djakarta, women with some education and/or technical skills are finding employment in multinational semiconductor companies. This poses another kind of challenge to the social customs of traditional Malay or Indonesian culture. In this section, we shall briefly explore the cultural impact of two important facets of modern, urban Southeast Asian life: industrial development, especially multinational semiconductor businesses; and tourism.

The challenge to the traditional values and social customs of the people of Southeast Asia varies from country to country and area to area. Relatively isolated rural groups are more protected from such things as Western rock music blaring forth from highly amplified loudspeakers, aggressive Coca Cola distributors, baby milk formula advertisements, and the substitution of polyester cloth for home-spun cotton. Still, in cities and towns throughout the entire Southeast Asian region, one finds all of the above, as well as the changes in values and lifestyle that they suggest: less respect for traditional lines of authority; change in diet, childrearing patterns, and dress; and Westernization and secularization. To be sure, using Colgate toothpaste and drinking Coca Cola does not make a Javanese into an American; yet the use of these products challenges the more traditional Southeast Asian ways of life.

One of the areas most dramatically affecting Southeast Asian culture is tourism. Over ten million tourists visit East and Southeast Asia every year, and tourism now constitutes the largest sector of international trade. The tourist industry has become a major economic, political, and cultural force in Asia. It is thought of as a strategic industry by many Asian governments. Large budgets are allocated for national airlines, advertising, hotel construction, and other tourist-related enterprises. While traveling can promote cultural interchange and personal enrichment, current Southeast Asian tourism, dominated by large international corporate interests, has a questionable impact on the peoples and societies involved.

International hotels, the heart of mass tourism, are often owned by multinational hotel chains. In the Philippines, for example, over fifty percent of the hotels have multinational affiliation. Although the tourism associated with these hotels brings in foreign exchange, most jobs associated with the tourist industry are low-skilled and low paying. In addition, tourists usually exhibit a kind of luxury consumption far beyond the reach of most Southeast Asians (but one often emulated by the wealthy elites in the Asians' own countries).

(United Nations photo/N. Prince)

Economic development in Southeast Asia challenges the traditional cultural patterns of the people. Young people are being drawn away from the values demonstrated by these newly ordained monks.

Thus, tourism tends to promote a lifestyle only the richest can afford and widens the gap between the wealthy and the poor. The poor see the acquisition of material goods as a goal to be achieved. This, in turn, promotes credit buying of such luxury items as televisions and motorcycles and often leads to an irreversible indebtedness.

One of the most pervasive consequences of tourism is prostitution. It is estimated, for example, that in Manila there are over 100 thousand prostitutes, and nearly 300 thousand in Bangkok. In most cases these women come from a background of rural poverty. In Thailand, for example, they come from the northeastern and northern parts of the country, and in the Philippines from the poorer provinces of Leyte, Samar, and Cebu. The income earned from prostitution often not only supports the women involved but their impoverished relatives as well. In many cases, however, this income involves great personal cost. Prostitutes are often exploited, work in miserable conditions, and lose social respect—as in the Philippines, for example, where the codes of sexual morality are strict.

The economic development of Southeast Asia has challenged customary social roles and values in other ways as well. There is widespread employment of young women in multinational semiconductor firms in such places as Penang, Malaysia. Many of these firms are headquartered in California where the research, development, and initial manufacturing stages take place. Once the complicated electronic circuitry wafers are fabricated, they are sent to Asia where Asian women perform the labor-intensive, routine, intermediate assembly operations. An assembler peers through a microscope for seven to nine hours a day, bonding each chip with as many as fifty thin gold wires. Although this kind of industrial development has created thousands of jobs, critics argue that the companies deliberately employ women because their economic weakness and social subordination make them easier to control than men. Critics argue, further more, that the personnel policies of these industries are designed to play up feminine submissiveness and to divert attention from pay and working conditions by stressing female stereotypes and superficial consumption.

On the one hand, new economic roles for women have been created, raising their status and undermining the patriarchal structure which often makes family life oppressive for women. On the other hand, industry personnel policies which encourage Western manners and consumption habits often make it difficult for women workers to fit into their communities and families. This is a dilemma not easily resolved, and one which characterizes the kind of cultural revolution taking place in Southeast Asia as the result of new forms of economic development, the growth of Western-style urban centers, and the increased concern with material values based on a consumer mentality.

Throughout Southeast Asia, there have been various efforts to cope with this kind of cultural change. In Burma, General Ne Win attempted to eliminate non-Burman—especially Western—influences in the country. Conservative Islamic groups in Indonesia and Malaysia have sought to return to traditional, if not stereotypical, Islamic cultural values. Other countries have sought to emphasize the traditional values often associated with religion, although not at the expense of modernization. An example of the latter are the recent policies of Singapore's head of state, Lee Kuan Yew. Singapore's progress in the past decade has been remarkable. A stable hard-working community of nearly two and a half million people has been steadily progressing toward economic prosperity. Recently, however, the government has grown concerned about the increasing Westernization and materialism that have accompanied this stability and prosperity. To counter these developments, the prime minister has called for a return to the traditional Confucian value system imbedded so deeply in Chinese culture. Confucian ethics must now be taught in the secondary schools; young people are being urged to become more courteous and more religious. Attempts are being made to engender a sense of social responsibility and obligation among young Singaporeans. In tapping the Confucian heritage of the Chinese, therefore, Lee is trying to strengthen the moral fiber of the country in order to curb the problems stemming from affluence.

ATTITUDE TOWARD HISTORY

In the parts of Southeast Asia dominated by Hinduism and Buddhism, history was traditionally looked upon as being relatively unimportant. What was of real importance was the attainment of a goal which was beyond history—Nirvana. Everyday life was viewed as a realm characterized by suffering and by the constant round of rebirths which, ultimately, one hoped to escape. In other words, the drama of salvation was not acted out in history, as in the Biblical tradition, but ahistorically. One tried to overcome the burden of history in order to reach a state where suffering and the pain of rebirth were overcome.

In the West, we have viewed history as being created by God and as the place where the drama of personal salvation is acted out. According to the Biblical tradition, at the time of creation human beings were given responsibility for the governance of the world. This tradition enforced the idea that history and the individual's place in it were important. This Biblical tradition was reinforced and reinterpreted under the influence of evolutionary thought in the nineteenth century. Not only was history important, it could, with our help, become progressively better.

This Western attitude toward historical progress has played one of the most important roles in the cultural revolution in Southeast Asia. It has caused some Asian leaders to look upon their own cultures as being basically static and caught up in a cyclical view of time and history.

This view did not, in their opinion, allow for the changes their countries needed in order to develop. The Marxist idea of dialectical change has had a particular appeal to many of the Southeast Asian leaders influenced by the Western understanding of history. The influence of socialist ideology has led to a view which Southeast Asian leaders such as U Nu in Burma have called a "Buddhist Socialism."

Buddhist Socialism, as a political and economic ideology, is a good illustration of a new synthesis between Western and Asian world views. In brief, it maintains that some of the Western ideas of historical development must be joined to some of the traditional Buddhist ideas about man's place in the world. The result, said U Nu, would be a society which could accommodate the material needs of its members but would also inspire them to seek more than just material ends. U Nu offered a political philosophy which rejected the atheistic or antireligious side of Marxist socialism but which affirmed the possibility of the progressive development of an ideal state.

The viewpoint of U Nu and other Asian leaders like him has real merit. We in America may not espouse a Buddhist Socialism, but the idea that the organization of a society should allow a person to seek a higher or spiritual end is appealing. Westerners may be no more materialistic than the people of Asia. However, we have developed such a highly successful technological society that we may have endangered our own well-being. If we have created a society in which we no longer see beauty in a flower, cease to be inspired by a beautiful sunset, or fail to feel compassion then all of our scientific and technological successes have ended in failure.

4

THE FUTURE

Thus far, our study of Southeast Asia has been an examination of the past and the present. In conclusion, we shall briefly look at the future. Our effort here is not to make predictions about what will or will not happen in Southeast Asia. We have no crystal ball which enables us to see what Vietnam will be like in a decade, what role China will be playing in the area, or what America's stake will be in the long run. Nevertheless, the future fascinates us. It is natural that we look to the future after studying the past and the present. We will consider the tensions between tradition and change, the problems of national identity, the role of pan-institutions in the quest for nationhood, the place of dynamic leaders, and the relationships between Southeast Asia, the West, China, and Japan.

TRADITION AND CHANGE

Southeast Asia has responded in diverse ways to change. For example, in Chapter 1, we noted ways in which new influences were rejected, brought about accommodations, or provided real cultural transformation. These patterns were first established during the early period of strong Indian influence in the region, continued later in response to Islam and the West, and are still in existence today, as the new Southeast Asian nations try to cope with modernization and Westernization. One of the most serious problems of the future rests in the way Southeast Asia responds to change.

Most of Southeast Asia is rural. The organization of

society still runs along traditional lines. Modernization has only begun to erode traditional values and traditional structures such as the family. The urban areas, however, which tend to be the centers of political and economic power, are modernized and often Westernized. The leaders of Southeast Asian countries, moreover, tend to be people who have been educated in the West or in Western schools in Southeast Asia. The differences between the large cities and the rural areas only reflect the conflict between tradition and change.

The educated elites of Southeast Asia want their countries to take a place among the developed nations of the world. They are encouraging industrialization and other forms of change associated with modern economies and are experimenting with political forms inspired by Western models. Yet there are questions about how much and what kind of changes ought to occur in Southeast Asia. For example, in Burma the British did away with the institution of kingship in the nineteenth century. In Thailand, never dominated by a Western power, the king remains an important symbol of national identity. His position was deemphasized after the revolution of 1932, but since the late 1950s his ceremonial and symbolic importance has increased. Indeed, he played a critical role in resolving a major political crisis in 1973. In Cambodia, Prince Sihanouk continues to play an important role in the coalition opposing the Vietnamese-backed ruling regime. The monarchical and princely traditions in some Southeast Asian countries are strong. How should these particular traditions change in terms of the demands of the modern day? Should they be dispensed with where they still remain? Should they be restored in some way where they have been destroyed? What role should the traditions of the Buddhist king and Islamic prince play?

We can illustrate the problem of tradition and change with an example from our own culture. Most of our large urban areas have undergone extensive redevelopment. Ghettos and slums have been demolished, and high-rise apartments have been built in their place. A few years ago, this kind of redevelopment occurred with little question about its value. Today, however, wholesale resettlement of economically deprived people is seriously questioned. More attention is being given to forms of community organization, family structure, social mores, and the various services necessary for social groups to function properly. It has been recognized that to bring about change in a living environment while ignoring traditional patterns of neighborhood life may create more negative than positive results.

In a similar manner in Southeast Asia, change and development which ignore traditional patterns of culture must be seriously questioned. While Burma's present isolationism may not be the best road to follow, the other extreme is also dangerous. Thailand, for example, has for many years been very open to America and Americans. In recent years, however, Thai intellectuals have become critical of excessive Western influence in their country. Sulak Sivaraksa, one of the co-founders of the Asian Cultural Forum for Development, has formulated a progressive development program based on native models appropriate to Thailand's peasant population and traditional cultural values. In doing so, he has been critical of both Western capitalism and Marxist development programs.

The best kind of change or development in Southeast Asia will be the kind which takes into account the deep cultural traditions of the region. The most effective economic and political stability will grow from the area's ancient cultural roots. To the diversity and unity which characterizes Southeast Asia will be added new elements derived largely from the West. Southeast Asia will ignore earlier traditions only at great peril. A people will make a commitment to change only when they are convinced that the cultural traditions making them a people are not being destroyed. The changes Southeast Asian leaders hope to make must, therefore, be culturally-enhancing rather than culturally-destroying. It is for this very reason that the role of America in certain parts of Southeast Asia is being questioned.

PROBLEM OF NATIONAL IDENTITY

We have mentioned that the notion of the modern nation-state was largely a product of the colonial era. Before this era, countries or territories tended to be organized dynastically. With the emergence of larger territorial units based on the nation-state model, special problems arose. Of particular importance is the question of national identity. Part of the problem in achieving this is the existence of minorities within the boundaries of a nation-state. For example, in Burma there are sizable minority groups in the northern part of the country. One of these groups, the Karens, became so powerful after World War II that they almost succeeded in taking over the government. The Karens have their own distinctive cultural traditions that differ from the Burmese. Thus, even though they are part of the Burmese nation-state, their primary identity is with their own ethnic and cultural grouping. In most Southeast Asian countries, similar situations hold true. In northern Thailand, for instance, where guerrilla warfare is one of the daily facts of life, the forces fighting against the Thais are largely ethnic groups who have never felt a strong identity with Thailand as a nation. Also, many Malay Muslims live in the extreme southern portion of Thailand. They feel less identity with Thailand than with their neighbors farther to the south.

The minority problem is also aggravated by the presence of immigrant Indians and Chinese who have settled in Southeast Asia. We have already noted the influence India has had in much of the region and that of China in more selected areas. Many Chinese and Indians who have migrated into Southeast Asia have been absorbed into native populations. Often this merging has led to genuine cultural change.

Yet, throughout Southeast Asia there are both Chinese and Indian communities who have remained relatively distinct. Many of these people are recent arrivals. For instance, from the middle of the nineteenth century onwards, there was a large migration of Chinese workers to the modern agricultural and mining enterprises established by the Western colonial powers. They became important economic factors in many Southeast Asian countries. In fact, in a country such as Thailand, the Chinese control much of the wholesale and retail economy.

The largest Chinese populations have been in Malaysia, Indonesia, and Thailand. The recent history of each country has been significantly conditioned by the Chinese minorities. When the Federation of Malay became independent in 1957, the island-city of Singapore was excluded largely because of its predominantly Chinese population. In 1963, when the Federation of Malaysia was created, it included Malaya, Singapore, and the states of Sarawak and Saban on the island of Borneo. However, in 1965 Singapore was asked to leave the federation. Consequently, today Singapore is an independent city-state because it is basically Chinese. In Indonesia, the overthrow of Sukarno and the emergence of General Suharto in 1965 led to a mass persecution of the Indonesian Communisty Party (PKI), many of whom were Chinese. Literally hundreds of thousands of PKI members were massacred during late 1965 and early 1966. In Thailand, where Chinese have been better assimilated than in either Malaya or Indonesia, their pervasive economic role has often created resentment among the Thais. With the recognition of Communist China, the question of the place of overseas Chinese in Southeast Asia may take on new dimensions. Especially in Thailand, the Chinese could figure prominently in any significant political change. One scholar, speaking about the relationship of the Chinese communities to Southeast Asian nationalism, concluded,

... the presence of Chinese in Southeast Asia does not entail the subversion of national integrity, and ... the economic benefits which the Chinese have brought to Southeast Asia ... [should], in a just world, earn them more gratitude than jealousy.

Indians in Southeast Asia in the modern period have been less of a problem, partly because by and large they have not settled in such large numbers. Nevertheless, problems similar to the conflict between Chinese and native populations emerged, especially in Burma. In Rangoon in 1930, for example, there were anti-Indian riots which were the direct result of competition between Burmese and Indian workers. General Ne Win nationalized industries and banks, licensing only Burmese for retailing and wholesale marketing. Consequently, Indians have left Burma in large numbers. Over 150 thousand have departed since April 1963. In Malaya, nearly ten percent of the total population is Indian. The largest proportion of them are laborers on plantations and have not figured as prominently in the political and economic life of the country as have the Chinese and Malays.

The issue of national identity after the end of the colonial period suggests many potential problems. Not only do large tribal groups live in the hills of countries such as Thailand and Burma, but Chinese and Indian populations were brought to Southeast Asian countries during the colonial period. None of these groups have strong feelings of loyalty to the national governments of the territories in which they reside. Their loyalties are more communal than national. The question of how they are to be assimilated into the nation-state raises serious issues. During the colonial period, the presence of outside Western powers helped to guarantee a certain degree of peaceful coexistence. After independence, however, a host of problems rose, such as the issue of national language. For example, after the 1957 coup in Thailand, the government decreed that Chinese schools had to conduct all classes in Thai rather than Chinese, with the exception of classes in the Chinese language. The future stability of many parts of Southeast Asia, especially Malaysia, depends on the ability to balance communal and national loyalties.

POLITICAL LEADERSHIP

Prior to the colonial period, much of Southeast Asia was divided into dynastic states. Most of these states were ruled by hereditary families and the king was viewed as an extremely powerful figure. In Cambodia, for example, he was looked upon as a god-king. In Thailand today the king is viewed with a respect bordering on veneration even though real power is in the hands of a ruling elite dominated by the military. Perhaps because this tradition of powerful dynasties and godlike kings is so recent in the history of Southeast Asia, powerful individual political leaders hold one of the most important keys to future political stability. Three of the most important of these leaders have been Sukarno in Indonesia, U Nu in Burma, and Sihanouk in Cambodia. All of these men were especially effective in enhancing feelings of national identity by using traditional symbols, especially religion.

Both U Nu and Sihanouk evolved a political philosophy which they called Buddhist Socialism. U Nu, in particular, had the genius necessary to bridge tradition and modernization and to speak in terms that the majority of the Buddhist populace of Burma could understand. Yet he infused these traditional terms with concepts of Western political and economic ideology. He had the uncanny ability to present innovations as nothing but traditional Burmese ideas. He preached a socialistic doctrine of a classless society without want, in which all members would strive for moral and mental perfection. The political and economic structure was

U Nu of Burma blended traditional Burmese ideas with Western political ideology to promote feelings of national identity.

to provide the context in which the Burmese could practice Buddhism seriously.

Apparently, U Nu genuinely believed that religion would save his country. When the Karen insurgents were threatening Rangoon in 1948, he is reported to have taken a vow of sexual abstinence in the belief that his vow would have some effect on the outcome of the rebellion: "On July 20, 1948, when the insurrection was causing anxiety, I went into my prayer room and before the Holy Image [of the Buddha] took the vow of absolute purity, making a wish at that time that if I kept that vow, the insurgents would be confounded."[11] He pledged to make Buddhism the state religion, with the conviction that it would provide the ideals necessary to make Burma an ideal nation. His commitment to using Burmese beliefs and practices in order to unite his people will be important for the future of Southeast Asia.

In Indonesia, Sukarno was to become the most important leader for national independence. He played a leading role in the 1920s, was arrested by the colonial authorities in 1930, and became President of the Indonesian Republic in 1945. His speech, "Indonesia accuses," delivered after his arrest, became one of the rallying points of the Indonesian independence movement. An excerpt follows:

> . . . the essence of the conviction of the P.N.I. [Sukarno's Indonesian Nationalist Party] as it was written in the declaration of principle [is]: 'The Partai Nasional Indonesia has the conviction that the most important precondition for the reconstruction of Indonesian Society is National Freedom, and therefore the endeavor of the whole of the Indonesian nation must be directed first of all to National Freedom'. Deviating from the point of view of many other political partices which teach: 'Reconstruct your economy, then freedom will come automatically'; deviating from the point of view of many other political parties which are of the opinion that freedom is the fruit of the [accomplished] recon-

struction of the economy, the P.N.I. says: 'Be zealous
in the cause of national freedom, for only through
national freedom can the Indonesian people bring
about complete national reconstruction'; thus it says
that complete national reconstruction is possible only
after the return of national independence. . . .[12]

In our own country we recognize the key role political
figures can play as exemplars of national values. Probably
the best illustration is John F. Kennedy. After his assassina-
tion, Kennedy became a martyr to the cause of high
individual and social ideals. Many young people, in particular, felt an acute personal loss, and the country seemed to
enter into a general emotional depression. Kennedy had a
particular style about him that attracted and inspired. He
projected an image of integrity and a commitment to the
highest ideals of the nation. No political leader since his time
has been so successful in projecting this image. The idealized
leader which Kennedy became for many people illustrates
the central role that can be played by political leaders in
Southeast Asia.

INTRAREGIONAL DEVELOPMENTS

The growing interconnectedness and interdependence of
the world is an ever-increasing fact of life. Americans eat
bananas grown in Brazil and drink tea from Sri Lanka;
Singapore residents view television programs beamed from
an American telecommunications satellite; followers of the
Hindu teacher Swami Bhaktivedanta might be found in the
Chicago O'Hare Airport; AFS students from Thailand may
attend American high schools. The future of Southeast Asia
reflects this same "one world" reality in both general and
particular ways. In the last few years, for example, two
significant intraregional connections have developed: One is
the Indochina region dominated by Vietnam, (i.e., Vietnam,
Cambodia, Laos); and the other is the alliance among

Thailand, the Philippines, Singapore, Malaysia, and Indonesia known as ASEAN (Association of Southeast Asian Nations).

ASEAN was founded in 1967 to increase cooperation in the areas of economic growth and social progress. There were efforts to break down trade barriers, expand exports, and stabilize prices. After 1976, however, in response to the increasing dominance of a communist Vietnam in Indochina, the ASEAN nations moved in a political direction to secure Southeast Asia as a "Zone of Peace, Freedom and Neutrality," a role played earlier by an alliance known as SEATO (Southeast Asia Treaty Alliance) that was supported by the United States and included Australia and New Zealand. Economically and politically, ASEAN is of interest to the United States. Politically, the alliance acts as a balance to the communist powers; agriculturally, the ASEAN nations are a part of the world commodity market controlled by a half-dozen Western transnational corporations. One of the most important of these corporations is the American firm of Gulf and Western. While the multinationals have opened up new production and marketing opportunities, local economies geared to production of exports run the risk of undermining a balanced agricultural growth essential to the needs of the majority peasant population.

The other major intraregional grouping is dominated by Vietnam and, indirectly, by the Soviet Union, which has supported Vietnam with extensive economic and military aid. Not only has a single Southeast Asian state become a dominant power for the first time in the post-independence period, it has called on the revolutionary forces in countries like Thailand and Malaysia to overthrow their ruling regimes. The threat of Vietnam is real. With a population of over fifty million and an army of 650 thousand it ranks as the Communist Bloc's third-largest country and the fourth-largest military force in the world. Indeed, its military strength is greater than the combined totals of all the

POPULATION DENSITY IN SOUTHEAST ASIA

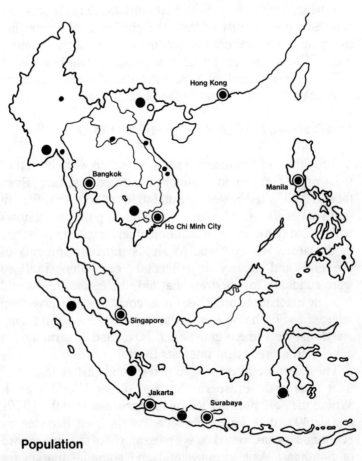

Population

- ◉ over 1,000,000
- ● 500,000 - 1,000,000
- ○ 250,000 - 500,000
- • 100,000 - 250,000

A number of major urban centers have become the focus of Japanese technical and development efforts.

ASEAN nations. In addition to a powerful military, Vietnam also has the most stable and cohesive leadership of any of the Southeast Asian states. Still, Vietnam has internal economic problems and it must address the challenge of thoroughly integrating the northern and southern halves of the country. Hopefully, a political balance of power in Southeast Asia will be achieved, and each nation will be allowed to develop in peace and cooperation to the benefit of all.

SOUTHEAST ASIA AND THE WORLD

The future of Southeast Asia is bound up with the rest of the world. The war in Vietnam illustrated that fact. Even though the United States now maintains a "lower profile" in that part of the world, our economic and political interests will probably mean a continuation of an American presence in the area. We continue to give significant amounts of economic and military aid to Thailand and Indonesia. If we were suddenly to withdraw that aid, the entire area would become much more unstable. Other countries also have deep interests in Southeast Asia. India and China have had a long-standing involvement in the area. Japan and Australia have developed more recent interests there.

The Japanese attempted to make Southeast Asia part of their "Asian Co-Prosperity Sphere" during World War II. Where they did not succeed by military means in the 1930s and 1940s, they have succeeded in the past decades by economic means. Bangkok is one example of the importance of Southeast Asia as an actual and potential market for Japan. Most of the cars on the crowded Bangkok streets are Japanese, and the bulk of electrical appliances are made in Japan. There are even Japanese department stores in Bangkok. It is clear that Japanese business interests are deeply involved in Southeast Asia.

Japan's influence in Southeast Asia, however, may well be strongest in the area of technical advice and development.

The Japanese have constructed a highly industrialized and technically trained nation-state. They are now playing an important role in the technical and industrial development of Southeast Asia. In the future, Japan will be important in Southeast Asia not as an exporter of Japanese-made goods but as an exporter of Japanese talent and expertise. Whereas the West has been the primary model for economic development up to the present, it may well be that Japan will assume that role.

China's role in Southeast Asia is more uncertain. China has continued to play an important role in Vietnam, even after the end of the Vietnam War. Politically, China may figure in a significant way in revolutionary movements in Thailand and Malaysia. China's most crucial role, however, may be more ideological than practical. The example of Chairman Mao still looms large. He was perhaps the most impressive Asian leader in the modern period. He effectively united a nation badly torn apart by the economic policies of Western colonial powers and by a devastating war. His revolutionary ideology is bound to influence the political future of Southeast Asia.

It would be a misconception, however, to assume that most Southeast Asian countries are on the verge of a revolution sponsored both ideologically and materially by the People's Republic of China (PRC). There are many types of governments in the region, ranging from military dictatorships to parliamentary democracies, and most of them have a reluctant and fearful attitude toward the PRC. China stands as the most powerful near-Asian neighbor; and there is the realization among the Southeast Asian nations that, with China's changing international fortunes, relationships with their giant neighbor must improve. However, there is fear of Chinese dominance, and for this reason the West, particularly America, is looked upon as a balance to that power. In terms of the balance of power in Southeast Asia, the United States will continue to play a critical role.

Although we may "lower our profile" for the well-being and development of Southeast Asia and other developed nations, we should offer aid when it is in the best interests of the countries involved. With our increasing awareness of global problems must come the realization that these problems can be solved only by global cooperation.

Our journey through Southeast Asia has been all too brief. We have, within the limits of our study, tried to develop an appreciation for the cultural traditions of the region. We have looked at developments in the colonial and modern periods from a perspective of negation, accommodation, and trans-formation. We have often referred to analogous problems within our own country or to relevant personal questions. The problems of Southeast Asia are, in part, our problems. The dynamics of tradition and change are faced by all of us in daily living. Hopefully, we can cope more successfully with some of these problems by knowing more about other cultures and civilizations.

QUESTIONS
FOR DISCUSSION

Chapter 1

QUESTIONS FOR DISCUSSION

1. What are some of the relationships between physical geography and climate, and social and economic patterns in the United States? How has geography and climate influenced the development of Southeast Asia?

2. What major ethnic groups have influenced the development of American culture? How have they influenced it? Do you see any general correspondences or differences in the way Indians or Chinese influenced Southeast Asia?

3. Traditional societies like most of those in Southeast Asia prize festivals. They serve to unite communities around common activities and goals. What are some of the major festivals of our own society? What importance do they have for you? For your community? Are they becoming more or less important? Why?

4. What, in your opinion, was the "greatest moment" in American history? What values about America did that moment illustrate? With the help of some additional reading about a particular Southeast Asian country discuss that country's "greatest moment" and the values it illustrates.

Chapter 2

QUESTIONS FOR DISCUSSION

1. How would you characterize the "American way of life"? What have been some of the recent challenges to this way of life? Are there any similarities to the challenges Southeast Asian countries currently face?

2. Who were the major European powers that dominated Southeast Asia in the nineteenth century? What are some of the similarities and differences between their presence in the region then and America's presence in the last decade?

3. Why did Southeast Asian countries desire to be independent from Western powers? Do you see any parallels between these independence movements and recent revolutionary movements in the West such as the IRA in Ireland or the Black separatist movement in this country? Others?

4. The effects of colonialism are often seen as entirely negative. Discuss some of the positive aspects of the Western presence in Southeast Asia.

Chapter 3

QUESTIONS FOR DISCUSSION

1. Have a conversation with a foreign student in your school about the ways in which America has influenced his or her values, outlook on life, and lifestyle. Or, if a new student has entered your school from a different part of the country, have him or her discuss some of the difficulties of

adjusting to new patterns of life. What are some of the ways in which Western culture has affected Southeast Asia?

2. How has your schooling affected your intellectual and social development? Should American schools be more involved in the process of development? In what ways did education affect the development of Southeast Asia?

3. Religion is considered to be one of the most stabilizing elements of a particular culture. What are the major religions of Southeast Asia and how have they been important in the development of the region? Has religion in America been only a conservative force?

4. Discuss some of the central teachings of Buddhism. How do they compare and/or contrast with the Judaeo-Christian tradition?

Chapter 4

QUESTIONS FOR DISCUSSION

1. Who were some of the great heros of the movements toward national independence in Southeast Asia (see also Chapter 2)? Why were they successful? Are there comparable figures in the Western Hemisphere today?

2. What are some of the major minorities in Southeast Asia today? How do they challenge the problem of national identity? Is there an American identity? If so, does it create conflicts with the larger minority groups living in America? How might they be resolved?

3. America continues to face major foreign policy questions regarding Southeast Asia. Some Americans simply want to get out of the region "lock, stock, and barrel"; others

argue that we need to maintain a strong force in order to block the communist advance. What do you think United States policy in Southeast Asia should be?

4. Southeast Asia, like much of the rest of the world, seems to be a region in transition. Discuss some of the major patterns these changes are taking. How would you apply them to your own society?

NOTES

(Chapter 1)

1. L.A. Peter Gosling, "Geography and the Resource Base for Economic Development," mimeograph.

(Chapter 2)

2. Harry J. Benda, and John A. Larkin, *The World of Southeast Asia: Selected Historical Writings* (New York: Harper and Row, 1967) pp. 128 and 129.

3. *Ibid.,* p. 136.

4. *Ibid.,* p. 184.

5. *Ibid.,* p. 194.

6. Rupert Emerson, "Paradoxes of Asian Nationalism," in *Man, State and Society in Contemporary Southeast Asia,* ed. Robert O. Tilman (New York: Praeger Publishers, 1969), p. 250.

7. D.W. Fryer, "The Million City," in *Ibid.,* p. 73.

(Chapter 3)

8. Robert O. Tilman, "Education as Political Development in Malaysia," in *Ibid.,* p. 231.

9. *Ibid.,* p. 232.

10. Walpola Rahula, *What the Buddha Taught* (New York: Grove Press, 1974), p. 88.

(Chapter 4)

11. *The Nation,* October 26, 1958, quoted in Richard Butwell, *U Nu of Burma* (Palo Alto: Stanford University Press, 1963), p. 65.

12. Benda and Larkin, *The World of Southeast Asia,* p. 191.

GLOSSARY

Angkor Wat One of the greatest religious monuments of the Khmer Empire, dating from the twelfth century.

Anwratha Founder of Pagan, the first major Burmese capital, around 1044 A.D.

ASEAN (Association of Southeast Asian Nations) Founded in 1967, it includes Thailand, the Philippines, Singapore, Malaysia, and Indonesia.

Aung San A leader of the Burmese nationalist movement who was assassinated in 1948.

Austro-Asiatic Neolithic peoples, possibly of a Mongoloid type, who inhabited the Southeast Asian mainland in the prehistoric period.

Borobodur A famous Buddhist architectural monument in Java, dating from the middle of the ninth century.

Brahmin The title given to the highest Hindu caste; originally associated with a priestly function. Often translated as "priest."

Chams An Austronesian-speaking people who inhabited an Indianized state (Champa), located in southern Vietnam, from about the second century A.D.

Datuk Seri, Dr. Mahathir Mohammad The fourth prime minister of Malaysia elected in 1982.

Federation of Malaya The alliance of Malay states that became a sovereign state in 1957 under the leadership of Tengku Abdul Rahman. This was followed in 1963 by a political union with Singapore and the Borneo states of Sabah and Sarawak. This union was called *Malaysia.* Two years later, Singapore withdrew from the union, becoming an independent state.

Funan An ancient Indianized state located in modern Kampuchea and part of southern Vietnam.

Hue A city in central Vietnam and its former capital.

Irrawaddy Burma's major river, traversing the country from the Patkai Range in the north to the Irawaddy Delta in the south.

Jayavarman VII The ruler of the Khmer Empire from 1181-1218 A.D.

Kampuchea Since 1973, the name of the nation-state formerly known as Cambodia.

Khmers Inhabitants of one of the most powerful states of mainland Southeast Asia from the second half of the sixth century to the fourteenth century.

Kuomintang Sun Yat-Sen's Nationalist Party, which governed mainland China from 1911 until the Communist revolution in 1949.

Lee Kuan Yew The leader of Singapore nationalism against the British and the present and first prime minister of Singapore, which has been an independent state since 1965.

Mahayana Buddhism One of the major divisions of the Buddhist tradition, associated primarily with East Asia (i.e., China, Korea, and Japan).

Majapahit A major dynastic power from the thirteenth century to the fifteenth century, based in Sumatra.

Marcos, Ferdinand President of the Philippines, elected in 1965; he was reelected in 1969 and declared martial law in 1972.

Mekong One of Southeast Asia's major rivers, flowing through Laos and Cambodia and emptying into the South China Sea off the southern coast of Vietnam.

Menam Chao Praya The major river of Thailand's central plain.

Minh, Ho Chi The leader of the Vietnamese nationalist movement against the French and president of the Democratic Republic of Vietnam.

Mon An Austroasiatic-speaking people of Burma and Thailand who flourished in those countries prior to the rise of the powerful Burmese and Thai states in the eleventh and twelfth centuries.

Ne Win The prime minister of Burma from 1962 to the present.

Osmena, Sergio The first speaker of the Philippine Assembly, elected in 1907.

Pagan Capital of and name for the high civilization that existed in Burma between the eleventh and fourteenth centuries.

PKI (Partai Kominis Indonesia) The Communist Party of Indonesia.

Pol Pot The pseudonym for Saloth Sar, a leader of the Cambodian Communist movement. Prime Minister of Kampuchea from 1975 until his overthrow in 1979.

Pyus A Tibeto-Burman speaking people who founded one of the early kingdoms (about the sixth century A.D.) in Burma.

Quezon, Manuel Leader of the Nationalist Party in the Philippines in the early twentieth century.

Rizal, Jose (1861-1896) Leader of the Philippine nationalist movement against the Spanish.

Sailendra An Indianized state, centered in Java and dating from the second half of the eighth century.

Sarekat Islam An Indonesia Muslim organization founded in 1912. It was important in the early nationalist movement.

Siddhartha Gotama The young prince who became known as the Buddha, and, hence, the founder of Buddhism.

Suharto The prime minister of Indonesia from 1966 until the present.

Sukarno A major leader of Indonesia's nationalist movement and prime minister until 1966.

Sun Yat-sen (1866-1925) Leader of the revolution that overthrew Manchu rule in China in 1911.

Suryavarman II The ruler of the Khmer Empire, from 1113 to around 1150 A.D. Sponsor of the building of Angkor Wat.

Swidden Agriculture A shifting form of cultivation in which fields are cleared and burned, planted for a few years, and then allowed to lie fallow before subsequent cultivation.

Theravada Buddhism One of the major divisions of the Buddhist tradition associated primarily with Sri Lanka and Southeast Asia.

U Nu The prime minister of Burma from 1948 to 1962.

Vessantara The prince-hero of a Buddhist morality fable popular in Southeast Asia.

SUGGESTED RESOURCE
MATERIALS
*Available in paperback

Bibliography on Southeast Asia is extensive. Books on many subjects may treat the entire area or focus on particular countries. Two helpful reference works are: Kennedy G. Tregonning. *Southeast Asia: A Critical Bibliography*. Tuscon: University of Arizona Press, 1969; and D.G.E. Hall, ed. *Atlas of Southeast Asia*. New York: St. Martins Press, 1964.

CHAPTER 1

Bibliography includes general histories and geographies, studies of particular Southeast Asian countries, and a variety of sources on the cultures of Southeast Asia.

Cady, John F. *Southeast Asia: Its Historical Development*. New York: McGraw-Hill, 1962.
A basic historical treatment of the entire region. Particularly good on later periods.

*_____. *Thailand, Burma, Laos and Cambodia*. (New York: Prentice Hall, 1966.
An excellent guide for the general reader to countries bound together by a common Buddhist religious heritage.

Coedes, George. *The Making of Southeast Asia,* trans. H.M. Wright. Berkeley and Los Angeles: University of California Press, 1966.
An outline sketch of the cultural history of mainland Southeast Asia by one of the major archaeologists and cultural historians of the region. Especially useful for its discussion of the founding of the early kingdoms.

Corpuz, Onofore D. *The Philippines.* New York: Prentice Hall, 1966.
> A useful general history emphasizing political developments.

Covarrubias, Miguel. *Island of Bali.* New York: Alfred Knopf, 1936.
> A volume beautifully illustrating the arts, dances, music, and drama of one of the world's most fascinating islands.

Crawford, Ann. *Customs and Culture of Vietnam.* Rutland, Vt.: Tuttle, 1966.
> A book which occasionally errs but is crowded with facts about the country, the people, their religions, education, customs, art, festivals, and legends.

DeYoung, John. *Village Life in Modern Thailand.* Berkeley: University of California Press, 1955.
> A detailed study of the social, religious, and agricultural patterns of the villages of northern Thailand.

Dobby, *Ernest H.G. Southeast Asia,* eleventh edition. London: University of London Press, 1973.
> A basic text of the environmental conditions and human adaptations in the countries of Southeast Asia.

Fisher, C.A. *Southeast Asia, A Social, Economic and Political Geography.* New York: E.P. Dutton, 1964.
> Chapters 1 and 2 discuss the physical and biogeological environment; Chapters 3 and 4 treat the pre-Western ethnic and political development of the region.

*Hall, D.G.E. *A History of Southeast Asia,* second edition. New York: St. Martins Press, 1964.
> The standard history of Southeast Asia. Invaluable as a reference work.

Harrison, Brian. *Southeast Asia: A Short History,* third edition. New York: St. Martins Press, 1966.
> The standad short history of the region, a useful introduction and well-balanced.

Htin Aung, U. *Burmese Folk Tales.* London: Oxford University Press, 1948.
> Some seventy-five tales organized under four headings: animals, romantic stories, wonder, and humorous tales.

Insor, D. *Thailand: A Political, Social and Economic Analysis.* New York: Frederick A. Praeger, 1963.

A standard handbook on Thailand.

Kartin. R.O. *Letters of a Javanese Princess.* New York: Norton, 1964.

English translations of the letters of a nineteenth century Javanese princess describing the cultural milieux of the times.

Keith, Agnes. *Bare Feet in the Palace.* Boston: Little, Brown, 1955.

A sympathetic report of living conditions among the native Filipinos in the barrios, villages, and jungle.

*Keyes, Charles F. *The Golden Peninsula. Culture and Adaptation in Mainland Southeast Asia.* New York: Macmillan Publishing Co., 1977.

The best available one-volume study of the cultures and societies of contemporary mainland Southeast Asia.

Khang, Mi. *Burmese Family.* Bloomington: Indiana University Press, 1962.

A delightful, autobiographical look at the family life of an early twentieth century Burmese girl.

Lebay, Frank, and others. *Laos: Its People, Its Society, Its Culture.* New York: Taplinger, 1960.

One of the volumes in the Human Relations Area Files series published through Yale University.

LeMay, Reginald. *The Culture of Southeast Asia.* London: George Allen & Unwin, 1956.

A discussion of the art of ancient and classical Southeast Asia with particular emphasis on the mainland.

_____. *Siamese Tales, Old and New.* London: Noel Douglas, 1930.

Tales that help to illustrate the Thai character.

McVey, Ruth T., ed. *Indonesia.* New York: Taplinger, 1963.

A reliable reference work.

Osborne, Milton. *Southeast Asia: An Introductory History.* Sydney: George Allen and Unwin, 1979.

An outline of the most important events and developments in Southeast Asia to explain why the area is as it is today.

Schutz, G. *Vietnamese Legends.* Rutland, Vt.: Tuttle, 1965.
Legends that give insight into the character and values of the
Vietnamese.

Steinberg, David L., *et al. Cambodia: Its People, Its Society,
and Its Culture.* New Haven: Human Relations Area Files
Press, 1957.
A standard handbook of history, economics, politics, and
society.

Wales, H.G. *The Making of Greater India,* second revised
edition. London: Bernard Quaritch Ltd., 1961.
Occasionally disputes Coedes's interpretations. Especially
useful for the pattern of cultural borrowing from India.

*Williams, Lea E. *Southeast Asia, A History.* New York: Oxford,
1976.
A recent historical study of Southeast Asia, focusing on
historical themes and currents rather than individuals and
events and particularly on the theme of unity within diversity.

CHAPTER 2

*Allen, Richard. *A Short Introduction to the History and Politics
of Southeast Asia.* New York: Oxford University Press,
1970.
Focuses on the political history of colonial and modern
periods of Southeast Asia. Factual but readable.

*Bastin, John, and Harry J. Benda. *A History of Modern
Southeast Asia, Colonialism, Nationalism and Decolo-
nialization.* Englewood Cliffs: Prentice-Hall, 1968.
More interpretation than the Allen volume. Part II on the
Southeast Asian response to the West in Southeast Asia is
especially useful.

*Benda, Harry J., and John A. Larkin. *The World of Southeast
Asia, Selected Historical Readings.* New York: Harper &
Row, 1967.
Pattern of organization similar to the Bastin and Benda
volume. A useful companion sourcebook.

*Butwell, Richard A. *Southeast Asia Today—and Tomorrow: A
Political Analysis,* revised edition. New York: Praeger,
1964.

A contemporary survey of the rapidly changing political developments within the region. Somewhat outdated but still valuable.

Cady, John. *A History of Modern Burma.* Ithaca: Cornell University Press, 1958.
A standard history of the country. "The Pivot for modern historical studies of Burma."

*Fall, Bernard. *The Two Vietnams: A Political and Military Analysis,* third revised edition. New York: Praeger, 1966.
A survey of the complicated French-Vietminh-Vietnam-American involvement in the region.

*_____. *Vietnam Witness: 1953-1966.* New York: Praeger, 1966.
Points out the follies of French, Vietnamese, and Americans.

Hunter, Guy. *Southeast Asia: Race, Culture and Nation.* Oxford: Oxford University Press, 1966.
The interaction of cultural, ethnic, and racial sectors of Southeast Asia within the perspectives of modernization and nation building.

Kahin, G. McT., ed. *Government and Politics of Southeast Asia,* second revised edition. Ithaca: Cornell University Press, 1969.
Major coverage of every country in Southeast Asia. Indispensible treatment.

McAlister, John T. *Vietnam: The Origins of Revolution.* New York: Alfred A. Knopf, 1969.
Deals with development of Vietnamese nationalism.

McGee, T.G. *The Southeast Asian City.* New York: Praeger, 1967.
A social geography of the major cities of Southeast Asia.

Mulne, R.S. *Government and Politics in Malaysia.* Boston: Houghton Mifflin Co., 1967.
Most comprehensive treatment of Malaysian politics.

*Neher, Clark D. *Politics in Southeast Asia.* Cambridge, MA: Schenkman Publications, 1981.
A study of the diverse nature of Southeast Asian politics according to shared patterns and themes.

*Steinberg, David J., ed. *In Search of Southeast Asia, A Modern History.* New York: Praeger, 1971.
One of the most recent books dealing with the modern history of Southeast Asia. Organized both regionally as well as country by country.

Vandenbosch, Amry, and Richard Butwell. *The Changing Face of Southeast Asia.* Lexington: University of Kentucky, 1966.
A concise account of recent developments in Indonesia, Malaysia, Philippines, Vietnam, Laos, Cambodia, Burma, and Thailand.

*Wilson, David. *Politics in Thailand.* Ithaca: Cornell University Press, 1962.
A study of contemporary political patterns with emphasis on kingship, national leadership, military, and political organization.

CHAPTER 3

Bellah, Robert N., ed. *Religion and Progress in Modern Asia.* New York: The Free Press, 1965.
Examines the role of religion in changing cultural patterns of Southeast Asia.

Burling, Robbins. *Hill Farms and Padi Fields: Life in Mainland Southeast Asia.* Englewood Cliffs: Prentice-Hall, 1966.
An explanation of the cultural changes over two millenia affecting the pattern of life in mainland Southeast Asia villages.

*Fitzgerald, Francis. *Fire in the Lake: The Vietnamese and the Americans in Vietnam.* Boston: Little and Brown and Co., 1972.
A Pulitzer Prize-winning study of American involvement in Vietnam.

Frederic, Louis. *The Temples and Sculpture of Southeast Asia.* London: Thames and Hudson, 1965.
A beautiful picture book that tells more about religion in Southeast Asia than a thousand words.

Geertz, Clifford. *The Religion of Java.* Glencoe, Ill.: The Free Press, 1960.

A detailed study by America's foremost anthropologist of Indonesian culture.

Hanh, Thich Nhat. *Vietnam, The Lotus in the Sea of Fire.* London: SCM Press, 1967.

A passionate account of the Vietnam crisis by a Buddhist monk.

Huq, Muhammad S. *Education and Development Strategy in South and Southeast Asia.* Honolulu: East-West Press, 1965.

The basic role in development of education analyzed in reference to two Southeast Asian countries.

Landon, Kenneth. *Southeast Asia: Crossroads of Religion.* Chicago: University of Chicago Press, 1949.

Outlines the ways in which cultural patterns were influenced by Buddhism, Islam, and Confucianism.

Nash, Manning. *The Golden Road to Modernity: Village Life in Contemporary Burma.* New York: Wiley, 1965.

Fascinating changes in the villages of Upper Burma.

Osborne, Milton. *Before Kampuchea: Prelude to Tragedy.* Sydney/Boston: Allen and Unwin, 1979.

A study of Cambodia prior to its transformation as a Communist state.

Schecter, J. *The New Face of Buddha, Buddhism and Political Power in Southeast Asia.* Tokyo: Westerhill, Inc., 1967.

A reporter's view of the role of Buddhism in recent developments in Southeast Asia.

Sigmund, Paul, ed. *Ideologies of the Developing Nations.* New York: Praeger, 1963.

Theories of state taken from speeches of their leaders including Sukarno and U Nu.

Swearer, Donald K. *Buddhism in Transition.* Philadelphia: Westminster Press, 1969.

A brief look at Buddhism, nationalism, and cultural revolution in Southeast Asia.

Tilman, Robert O. *Man, State and Society in Contemporary Southeast Asia.* New York: Praeger, 1969.

An invaluable collection of essays covering such topics as nationalism, minorities, cities, and international organizations.

CHAPTER 4

Armstrong, John P. *Sihanouk Speaks*. New York: Walker, 1964.

An uncritical study. Contains some rather poorly edited speeches.

Putwell, Richard. *U Nu of Burma*. Palo Alto: Stanford University Press, 1963.

A careful and sympathetic portrait of U Nu.

Darling, Frank C. *Thailand and the United States*. Washington, D.C.: Public Affairs Press, 1965.

Some prescriptive advice and warnings for both Thailand and the United States.

Golay, Frank H., ed. *The United States and the Philippines*. Englewood Cliffs: Prentice-Hall, 1966.

Essays prepared for the 1966 meeting of the American Assembly.

Gordon, Bernard K. *Toward Disengagement in Asia: A Strategy for American Foreign Policy*. Englewood Cliffs: Prentice-Hall, 1969.

A useful study in the area of international politics and foreign policy.

Legge, John D. *Sukarno: A Political Biography*. New York: Praeger, 1972.

One of the standard studies of Indonesia's great nationalist leader.

Rosenberg, David. *Marcos and Martial Law in the Philippines*. Ithaca: Cornell University Press, 1979).

A study of the authoritarian nature of the Marco regime.

Silverstein, Joseph. *Burmese Politics: The Dilemma of National Unity*. New Brunswick: Rutgers University Press, 1980.

The most up-to-date study of the Burmese political situation.

Wrightman, D. *Toward Economic Co-Operation in Asia*. New Haven: Yale University Press, 1963.

A study of the work of the United Nations Economic Commission for Asia and the Far East.

ADDITIONAL BIBLIOGRAPHIC NOTES

I. Periodicals

There are a variety of periodicals which deal with Southeast Asia. Some of the most useful are: *Journal of Asian Studies* (Ann Arbor: Association for Asian Studies); *Asian Survey* (Berkeley: Institute of Pacific Relations); *Pacific Affairs* (Vancouver Institute of Pacific Relations); *Journal of Southeast Asian History* (University of Singapore); *Journal of the Siam Society* (Bangkok); *France-Asia* (Saigon & Tokyo); *Indonesia* (Cornell University); *Asian Studies* (University of the Philippines).

In addition to the above most Southeast Asian Government Embassies publish some type of periodic literature.

INDEX